ST. ANDREWS

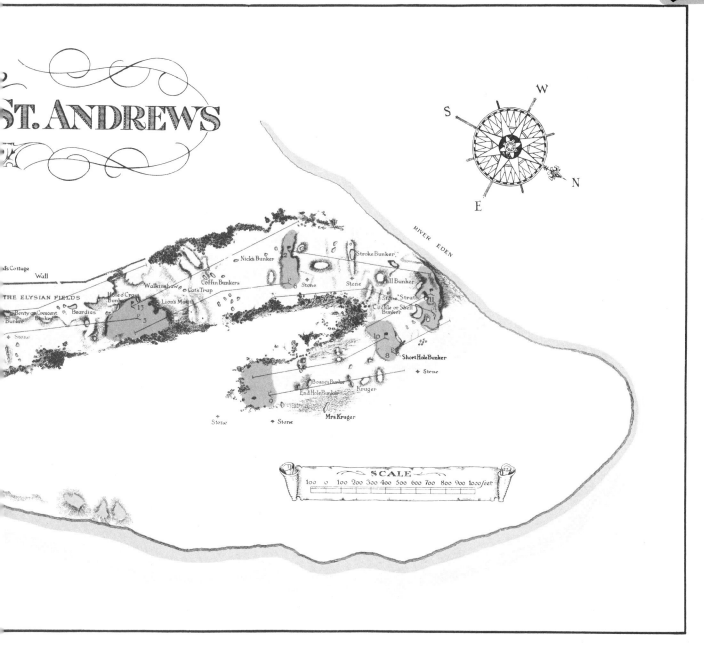

RIVER EDEN

Nick's Bunker

Stroke Bunker

Coffin Bunkers

Walkinshaw

Cat's Trap

Stone

Stone

Hill Bunker

ds Cottage

Wall

THE ELYSIAN FIELDS

Hole o'Cross Bunker

Lion's Mouth

Strath

Cockle or Shell Bunker

Benty or Crescent Bunker

Beardies

Stone

Short Hole Bunker

Stone

Boase's Bunker

Kruger

End Hole Bunker

Stone

Stone

Mrs Kruger

SCALE

100   0   100 200 300 400 500 600 700 800 900 1000 feet

S W E N

ST ANDREWS

Previous books by the author include

Newmarket

Journey Through Cornwall

The Old Inns of London

Life in Cambridge

Germany After the War

The Sunday Book

The Beauty of Woman

The London Season

People, Places and Pleasures

Collecting Staffordshire Pottery

Golf With Your Hands

Swing to Better Golf

Los Campeones de Tenis en Accion

The B.R.M. Story

Grand Prix World Championship

ST ANDREWS

Louis T. Stanley

W.H. ALLEN · LONDON

Copyright © 1986 Louis T. Stanley

Typeset by Phoenix Photosetting, Chatham
Printed and bound in Great Britain by
Mackays of Chatham Ltd, Chatham, Kent
for the Publishers, W.H. Allen & Co. Plc
44 Hill Street, London W1X 8LB

British Library Cataloguing in Publication Data

Stanley, Louis T.
  St. Andrews.
  1. Royal and Ancient Golf Club of St.
  Andrews———History
  I. Title
  796.352'06   GV969.R6

ISBN 0–491–03560–8

CONTENTS

INTRODUCTION

by
Ronald Alexander

Captain, Cambridge University Golf Team, 1953–54
Captain, Royal and Ancient Golf Club, 1980–81
Chairman, Professional Golfers Association, 1982–85

I FIRST MADE the acquaintance of Louis Stanley, then an Economist, at Cambridge after the War when I was at Clare College and he was at Emmanuel. We shared an interest in University golf and a particular fondness for St Andrews, which I had first come to know some twenty years earlier when my parents were sensible enough to rent a house there for the month of August each year.

I feel that I should immediately confess that I have loved St Andrews for as long as I can remember. I have read in this book that Mary, Queen of Scots regarded St Andrews as 'the most attractive town in her kingdom' – a view with which, needless to say, I concur wholeheartedly.

For many years now I have said that, if I were sentenced to play on one golf course for the rest of my life, I would without hesitation choose the Old Course. Louis Stanley has quite rightly written that the Old Course is 'the greatest of classics' and 'a precious possession, the ultimate golfing test of courage and skill'. It may not strike the golfer as such on his first encounter, but this is a case where familiarity breeds respect. I must have played some hundreds of rounds on the Old Course, and what amazes me is that even today I find something new or different about it each time I play there.

St Andrews is perhaps best known throughout the world as the home of golf, but there is much more to the town than that. It holds a most important place in the history of Scotland, and visitors today will be well rewarded by the sights of the ruined Cathedral and Castle – and the flourishing University, the oldest in Scotland.

I applaud Louis Stanley's inclusion of a chapter on 'Women Golfers at St Andrews'. Golf at St Andrews may be thought to be a predominantly male pursuit, but this is not entirely true. And if any 'golf widow' is fearful of coming to St Andrews, she should not be – it is a lovely town with everything to offer.

Louis Stanley has long won admiration for his writings on the game of golf. In this book his pen and camera have ranged widely. It makes fascinating reading for everyone, whatever his or her taste. He speaks with true affection of the town, the great Championships and matches, the great players who have won at St Andrews, many of whom he knows well, and, last but not least, the personalities and characters, of which I can say with certainty that there is still an abundance in St Andrews today. In every way *St Andrews* is an absorbing addition to the literature of the game.

This is Louis Stanley's 64th book. I look forward to the 65th which will equal Henry Cotton's record 65 at Royal St George's in the Open Championship of 1934!

CHAPTER 1

St ANDREWS

CHAPTER 1

St ANDREWS

THE GHOSTS OF the past speak eloquently from the top of the tall stone tower of St Rule set on its foundation of boulders. Climb the dark spiral with the wind whistling down the damp stairs and pigeons cooing, then look over the sheer drop at the remains of the loveliest of cathedrals. In imagination it is easy to re-people the decaying ruins. For some five hundred years the ascetic rules of the Augustinian Order, the richest monastic foundation in Scotland, were observed day after day as cowled monks went about their devotions before the various altars from dawn until compline. Some trace of those outpourings of faith must surely be impregnated in the stones.

It was at the High Altar in June 1538 that James V and the lovely Mary of Lorraine, daughter of the Duke of Guise were 'espousit with great glory' before the lords, spiritual and temporal. This talented young woman found St Andrews much to her liking, for after visiting the friaries and colleges, she told the provost and burgesses that 'she never saw so many fair personages of men, women, young babies and children, as she saw that day'. Her stay in the grey city lasted two years. She bore a son who died early and a daughter who became Mary, Queen of Scots. It was also here that Bruce stood at the consecration of the building. Much later the walls echoed to the denunciation by John Knox of 'the hellish priests, belly-gods and shavelings' in sermons that incited the rabble to plunder, ravage and destroy the fabric of the cathedral. Images, relics and treasures vanished, leaving a structure like the bones of a dead world. The aftermath was serious. Like Canterbury, St Andrews had become dependent on the pilgrims who for centuries had journeyed across Europe to the Shrine where miracles were wrought. How it all began is a strange story. Behind the beautiful bronze doors inset with silver of the striped cathedral of Amalfi and in the dimly lit crypt is the tomb where once a year the miracle of the 'manna di Sant Andrea' occurs as the glass phial held by the Archbishop becomes wet with fluid from the saint's bones. The man originally responsible for linking the venerable town of Amalfi with the old grey town of St Andrews was Cardinal Pietro Campuano.

After the Ascension, Andrew, the gentle brother of Simon Peter, who was the first disciple called by Our Lord, became the first missionary to the Muscovites and to Scythia, later returning to Jerusalem before embarking on a mission to Greece. Among his converts was the wife of the Roman governor of Patrae, who, furious that his wife had been converted, sentenced Andrew to be crucified. His hands and feet were not nailed, but bound with cords to make the agony more prolonged. The X-shaped cross was chosen by Andrew because he felt unworthy to die on the same type of cross on which Christ had suffered and died. The body was buried by the governor's wife. Later the bones were exhumed and taken to Constantinople to be placed alongside those of St Luke in the Church of the Apostles and remained so until 1208 when Cardinal Campuano offered the relics to his native town, Amalfi.

The Aberdeen Breviary takes up the story. According to the Scottish monks, the Cardinal gave only part of the skeleton to Amalfi. The custodian of the relics, by name St Regulus or St Rule, had a vision in which an angel instructed him to take three finger-bones, an arm-bone and a knee-cap of the saint to the western limits of the world and there found a city in honour of the apostle. The route outlined by the monks left much to be desired as regards accuracy. Nevertheless, the journey was made and the Shrine of St Andrew became famed for the miracles performed in its name. Thousands of pilgrims made the difficult passage as a votive tablet records: 'The bay and the shore of the sea though rough and boisterous, contains a most fertile country; this region, once poor, foul and desolate is now rich, beautiful and flourishing. Hither come to pray a crowd of men from the most distant regions – the loquacious Frenchman, the war-like Roman, the Flemish weaver, the uncivilised German, the Englishman, the Saxon, the Hollander, the naked Pict, the savage Angerian, and strangers from the Rhône and the Tiber come to seek the prayers of Saint Andrew.'

St Andrews had become to Scotland what Canterbury was to England. The thought of pilgrims praying before the relics in a shrine surrounded by a forest of burning tapers seems alien to the Scottish character, yet it created the ecclesiastical capital and the Patron Saint of Scotland. Religious fervour takes many forms. Reforming plunderers leave trails of destruction to the glory of God. Small wonder that their spirits seem ill at ease. The ghost of John Knox is said to frequent North Street, though why this particular street is difficult to imagine.

The Tower of St Rule. From the lead roof can be seen the Lomond Hills of Fife and the Sidlaw Hills beyond Dundee.

A figure in monk's robes has been seen in the Pends. The Haunted Tower by the cathedral lives up to the reputation fictionalised by W. T. Linskill. Hepburns Wall has a restive wraith. Sharp's coach has been heard near Lade Braes. Even the headless Darnley has made an appearance, but all pale into insignificance alongside the happenings in the ruined Castle that rises above the sea.

The Castle with its Bottle Dungeon and secret passage
has withstood battery from cannon, siege and storm
over the centuries.

The structure has withstood battering from cannon, siege and storms since Bishop Roger, son of the Earl of Leicester, built the walls on the cliffs in 1200. Its subsequent history is sullen and horrific. Today little is left except the gate-house, a secret passage and the nightmare Bottle Dungeon, roughly shaped like a bottle with the neck the only entrance. Victims were lowered by rope into a darkness more impenetrable than the blackest night. Death under such conditions must have been a relief. A catalogue of the cruelty inflicted in the name of Christ records that George Wishart, the Protestant Reformer and friend of John Knox, was burned to death at the stake in 1545 in front of the Castle where Cardinal Beaton sat and watched with reported satisfaction. Two months later revenge was taken by a group of sixteen men, led by John and Norman Leslie, William Kirkcaldy and James Carmichael, who planned a daring attack on a par with a twentieth-century SAS assault exercise. The timing was perfect. When the drawbridge was lowered to admit a relief force, they rushed the gate, killed the warder and headed for the Cardinal's apartments. The ambitious prelate, whose cruelty and immorality had become a byword, having seized supreme authority on the death of James V by naming himself Regent on the strength of a forged royal will, was given no mercy. He was killed almost ritually. The body was then slung over the Castle wall and suspended by a foot and an arm. It was a sacrilegious murder likened to that of Thomas à Becket. Catholics were horrified, Protestants jubilant. Reaction was immediate. The Castle was besieged, but the support of the English fleet promised by Henry VIII did not materialise. The assault launched by the Regent Arran did not succeed and the garrison held out for over a year until a fleet of sixteen warships anchored in the bay with *fleur-de-lis* on their sails. Under the command of an Italian, Leon Stronzius, cannon were mounted on the tower of St Salvator's College and on all high vantage points, even the cathedral walls. The pounding that followed led to a surrender. The defenders, including John Knox, were chained in galleys and taken to France. When the French troops entered the Castle, they found the body of Cardinal Beaton preserved in a solution of salt in the Bottle Dungeon.

Apart from the Bottle Dungeon, the Castle remains now look innocent of such violence, but visitors, particularly Americans, have a nose for blood. Lurid details are statistics to be noted. All is grist to the tourist's mill. Anywhere that has burnt martyrs, drowned witches, beheaded royalty, murdered clerics, destroyed monasteries and desecrated cathedrals is a bonus for those with a nose for graphic history. A further association strikes a gentler note. Of the many towns in Scotland associated with Mary Queen of Scots, almost all are associated with stress and intrigue. St Andrews is the exception, for here she could escape from the pressures of State.

The royal life was controversial and romantic. Her childhood was passed in France. At 16 she married the Dauphin to become Queen of France. A gold ducat struck for the wedding shows the outlined profiles of Mary and the Dauphin with the arched crown of Scotland suspended between them. Less than two years later she was widowed when Henry II died after being accidentally struck in the eye at a tournament, and she returned to Scotland as Queen after an absence of thirteen years. What happened afterwards is pure melodrama. Tussles at the outset with John Knox and the Scottish nobility were followed by the disastrous marriage to Darnley and his strange death. An engraving in the British Museum shows realistic likenesses of Henry, Lord Darnley and Mary at the time of her infatuation

Right:
The quadrangle of St Salvator's College.

with and marriage to her 19-year-old cousin which ended with his murder eighteen months later at Kirk o' Field. Then came her marriage to Bothwell, the main suspect, and the silver casket discovered after Darnley's death containing love letters from Mary to Bothwell and other documents incriminating the queen in the murder of her husband. Whether these were authentic or forgeries remains a conundrum of history, but they resulted in her lengthy imprisonment at the hands of Queen Elizabeth, culminating in the tangled Babington plot to free her, and finally her execution at the age of 44.

History has a detailed record of the development of this lovely, pleasure-seeking girl into a woman aged beyond her years when she came to die. In St Andrews we find clues as to what Mary Queen of Scots was really like and might have been. We know that she regarded St Andrews as the most attractive town in her kingdom. She was only nineteen when she arrived from France, and on her horseback tour she was the first lady in Scotland to ride side-saddle with a pommel. The itinerary included Linlithgow, where she was born; Stirling where she was crowned as an infant; Falkland where her father, James V, died; Perth and Dundee, but only in St Andrews was she able to get privacy. The haven was a pre-Reformation house near the Pends, built in 1523 by Hugh Scrymgeour, a wealthy merchant, and now part of St Leonard's School. Rather than the social delights of fashionable Edinburgh, she preferred the quietness of a panelled little room. From her bedroom, she looked on to a garden and trees where she studied Livy under the tutorship of George Buchanan, the principal of St Leonard's College, who had taught her in France, or she practised at the butts. A corner oriel extends gracefully from her bedchamber, where she prayed, possibly using the golden rosary, crucifix and prayerbook she carried to her execution and which she held on the steps of the scaffold when she spoke to the assembly 'with joyous

countenance', saying 'I have been brought before a company who will witness that I die a Catholic.' Against such a background, St Andrews offers a gentle vignette of the Queen. There used to be the ghost of a woman in dark clothing who moved through rooms, now the School library, into the garden. The wraith was seen by many people, but exorcism with bell, book and candle laid the spirit to rest.

St Andrews has a four-fold appeal. As ecclesiastical capital of Scotland, it has enough material to satisfy the appetite of any researcher; the historical aspect of the town can illuminate the background of controversial issues and events; the Royal and Ancient Golf Club is the focal point of the golfing world; in the old days pilgrims used to journey across Europe to the Shrine of St Andrew, and today the pilgrims come in even bigger numbers drawn by the appeal of the Old Course and the fact that St Andrews is the acknowledged home of the game.

The fourth attraction is the fact that St Andrews has the oldest University in Scotland. Had the Cathedral not been destroyed, together they would have been hailed as the Cambridge and Canterbury of Scotland. St Andrews is unique in Britain as a proud medieval foundation. It impressed Dr Johnson, who wrote, 'it seems to be a place eminently adapted to study and education, being situated in a populous yet a cheap country, and exposing the minds and manners of young men neither to a levity and dissoluteness of a capital city, nor to the gross luxury of a town of commerce, places naturally unpropitious to learning.' The words still apply.

At the outset, studies at St Andrews University were based on Paris as the ideal model. *Bajans*, or entering students, were often no older than five and were expected to know grammar well. Logic and rhetoric were the first hurdles, after that Aristotelian ethics, physics and metaphysics. Bachelorhood could be

The Cathedral where James V and Mary of Lorraine were married at the High Altar.

colleges of St Mary's and St Leonard's were based on it, as were King's and Marischal Colleges of Aberdeen, while the Universities of Edinburgh and Glasgow followed suit in varying degree. There were setbacks. During the Reformation, St Salvator's was reduced to eleven students, St Leonard's to ten, St Mary's the same, while in 1558 the entire University had only three students. Somehow they thrived on crisis. Even in recent years there was a threat of absorption by Dundee, but perseverance prevailed and men like Sir James Irvine then Chancellor of the University were able to consolidate, often with substantial financial help from American friends.

The University is small, but it is the right size for St Andrews. In term time the streets are sprinkled with students – scarlet gowns against grey stone. Young men in scarves and corduroys and jeans, girls, in slacks or tweeds. During the three years, memories are stored for the years ahead, recalling a temper of life that was leisured and purposeful. Many of the features never change. The background remains as grey and speckled as a piece of home-spun tweed. There will always be the stones of the ruined Castle and Cathedral, the Pends, men smoking an evening pipe as they lean on the white railings and watch golfers crossing the Swilcan bridge, the familiar outline of the Royal and Ancient clubhouse. There is about it a continuity of atmosphere and tradition that appeal equally to the visitor who returns. And if it rains, as often happens, and a grey mist envelops the Old Course from the bay, there is always the luxury of a traditional Scottish tea, be it in Rusacks, the Old Course Country Club, Hall of Residence or College Rooms.

achieved after eighteen months, and a licentiate after four years, followed immediately by a mastership. If ambition turned towards a doctorate of theology, eight more years of work were required. St Salvator's became the standard for higher learning in Scotland. The later

CHAPTER 2
THE ROYAL AND ANCIENT GOLF CLUB

CHAPTER 2
THE ROYAL AND ANCIENT GOLF CLUB

THERE WAS NOTHING cut and dried about the beginnings of the Royal and Ancient, no formal inauguration of a Club complete with name, premises, constitution and laws with elected office holders. It was an evolutionary process that began on 14 May 1754 when 'twenty-two Noblemen and Gentlemen being admirers of the ancient and healthfull exercise of the Golf' met and drafted certain Articles and Laws and formed themselves into 'The Society of St Andrews Golfers.' Little did they realise what would come of their deliberations and it seems wrong for these founder members to remain anonymous. We know their names. It is fitting to recall them as individuals.

The list is headed by Charles, 5th Earl of Elgin and 9th Earl of Kincardine; James, 4th Earl of Wemyss, Captain-General of the Royal Company, and first winner of the Silver Bowl, a competition inaugurated in 1720 by the Archers; Thomas, son of John, 9th Earl of Rothes, Equerry to the Prince of Wales, barrack-master of Scotland who represented Perth in Parliament; his brother, James, was an advocate, Sheriff Deputy of Fife; the Hon. Francis Charteris; Sir James Wemyss, Bart., Laird of Bogie; Lt-General James St Clair, a distinguished soldier who commanded the Royal Scots, was Quartermaster-General in Flanders in 1745, and who represented Fifeshire in Parliament; James Oswald of Dunnikier, an outstanding statesman who represented

HRH The Duke of Kent leaving the Royal and Ancient Clubhouse in 1938 with the Hon. John Lowther (left) and Colonel MacAllan.

Kirkcaldy Burghs in Parliament; Sir Robert Henderson, 4th Baronet of Fordell and Provost of Inverkeithing; David Young, remembered as the Professor who had proposed that the Honorary Degree of Doctor of Laws be conferred on Benjamin Franklin by the University of St Andrews. He was appointed to the Chair of Natural and Experimental Philosophy in the United College in 1747 after being a Professor in St Leonard's College; his brother, John Young, Professor of Moral Philosophy at the University for over forty years; James Lumsdain of Rennyhill, Provost of St Andrews for seven years from 1753; David Scot of Scotstarvit; Thomas Spens of Lathallan; Maurice Trent of Pitcullo; James Wemyss of Wemysshall; Walter Wemyss of Lathockar; John Bethune of Blebo; Henry Bethune of Clatto; James Cheap of Sauchie; Arthur Martin of Milston, and Robert Douglas, probably a St Andrews merchant. Such were the founder members, all keen golfers; some were also good archers.

The next step was to draw up a code of rules. *The Articles and Laws in playing the Golf* had been formulated eleven years earlier by the Company of Edinburgh, later the Honourable Company of Edinburgh Golfers, who played on the Links of Leith with Duncan Forbes of Culloden as their President. Their thirteen rules were adopted by St Andrews with only minor alterations:

1. You Must Tee your Ball within a Club Length of the hole.
2. Your tee must be upon the Ground.
3. You are not to Change the Ball which you Strike off the Tee.
4. You are not to Remove Stones, Bones or any Break Club for the Sake of playing your Ball Except upon the fair Green and that only within a Club Length of your Ball.
5. If your Ball come among Water, or any Watery filth, You are at Liberty to take Your Ball, and throwing it behind the hazard 6 yards at least, You may play it with any Club, and allow your Adversary a Stroke, for so getting out your Ball.
6. If your Balls be found any where touching one another, You are to lift the first Ball, till You play the last.
7. At holeing, You are to play your Ball honestly for the Hole, and not to play upon your Adversary's Ball, not lying in your way to the hole.
8. If you should lose your Ball, by its being taken up, or any other way You are to go back to the Spot where you Struck last, and drop another ball, and Allow your Adversary a Stroke for the Misfortune.
9. No Man at Holeing his Ball, is to be Allowed to Mark his way to the Hole with his Club or any thing else.
10. If a Ball be Stop'd by any person, Horse, Dog or any thing else, the Ball so Stop'd Must be played where it lyes.
11. If you draw your Club, in Order to Strike, and proceed so far in the Stroke as to be bringing down your Club; if then your Club shall break, in any way, it is to be accounted a Stroke.
12. He, Whose Ball lyes furthest from the Hole is Obliged to play first.
13. Neither Trench, Ditch, or Dyke made for the preservation of the Links, Nor the Scholars Holes or the Soldiers Lines, shall be Accounted a Hazard, But the Ball is to be taken out, Teed and played with any Iron Club.

Having become formally established, the founder members subscribed to a Silver Club for competition with entry open to players in Great Britain and Ireland, the winner to attach to it a silver ball with his name engraved on it. That proved to be Bailie William Landale, merchant in St Andrews, who won on 14 May 1754 and became the first Captain of the Club.

One drawback was the lack of a permanent meeting-place. At the outset, members met in Glass's Inn and dined on payment of a shilling. It was here that Boswell and Johnson enjoyed 'rissered Haddocks and mut' chops'. The site was later occupied by the Black Bull Inn in South Street in 1786. Lord Cockburn recalled a visit to this inn in *Circuit Journeys* and how the locals 'have a pleasure of their own, which is as much the staple of the place as old colleges and churches are. This is golfing, which is here not a mere pastime, but a business and a passion, and has for ages been so, owing probably to their admirable links. This pursuit actually draws many a middle-aged gentleman whose stomach requires exercise, and his purse cheap pleasure, to reside here with his family; and it is the established recreation of all the learning and all the dignity of the town. There is a pretty large set who do nothing else, who begin in the morning

The path in front of the Royal and Ancient Clubhouse was well patronised at the beginning of this century.

23

and stop only for dinner; and who, after practising the game, in the sea breeze, all day, discuss it all night. Their talk is of holes. The intermixture of these men, or rather the intermixture of this occupation, with its interests, and hazards, and matches, considerably whets the social appetite. And the result is, that their meetings are very numerous, and that, on the whole, they are rather a guttling population. However, it is all done quietly, innocently, and respectably; insomuch, that even the recreation of the place partakes of what is, and ought to be, its peculiar character and avocation.'

These words were written in 1844 but in many ways are still applicable. The Club, however, did not limit its gatherings to Glass's Inn, for there are references to meetings in The Bunch of Grapes and The Cross Keys. In 1835 the Union Club was inaugurated for the combined benefit of St Andrews Archers Club and the Golf Club in premises known as the Union Parlour on a site later occupied by the Grand Hotel, now Hamilton Hall, part of the University. The arrangement proved satisfactory until 1853 when it was decided that new premises should be built. The following year marked the opening of the Royal and Ancient Clubhouse and in 1876 the Royal and Ancient amalgamated with the Union Club.

Many of the landmarks in the historical background of the Royal and Ancient Club are linked with their famous trophies. The Silver Club was won by William Landale, but James Durham of Largo should be remembered for his winning score of 94 that remained unbeaten for 86 years. In 1806 a Gold Medal became part of the Autumn Meeting and was played for two days after the Silver Club. The first winner was Walter Cook, W.S., with a score of 100. In 1824 it was decided that the Silver Club would no longer be competed for but would go with the Captaincy, instead of the office being conferred on the winner. Five years earlier the Silver Club was replaced by a replica because after 65 years it was impossible to add any further silver balls to the club. In 1833 a Silver Club was presented to the Club by John Whyte-Melville of Strathkinness as a result of a survival bet made with Sir David Moncrieffe in 1820. The terms of the curious wager stipulated that on the death of one of them, the other should donate to the Club a Silver Putter on which the arms of the two parties were engraved. On the trophy the Gold Medals won at successive meetings should be hung in the same way as the silver balls were attached to the Silver Club.

Major J. Murray Belshes of Buttergask was instrumental in obtaining the King William IV Gold Medal in 1837 and a year later the Queen Adelaide Gold Medal, which on her wishes is worn by each Captain on all public functions during his term of office. Murray Belshes also succeeded in getting for the Club the Patronage of King William IV and the title of Royal and Ancient. Two years earlier Belshes had given the Club the Silver Cross of St Andrew which became the main scratch medal of the Spring Meeting. It was won for the first time in 1836 by James Condie of Perth with a score of 110. From 1837 the Gold Medal became the second scratch prize to the King William IV Medal at the Autumn Meeting. J. Stuart Oliphant was the first winner with 104, while O. T. Bruce of Falkland became the first Captain to wear the Queen Adelaide Medal.

In 1845 Colonel Playfair presented to the Club a Silver Medal on behalf of the Golfing Society of Bombay. It was made the second scratch prize at the Spring Meeting. William Buist was the first winner in 1846 with 111. The Royal Blackheath Club offered the Club in 1882 the George Glennie Gold Medal to mark this player's long and active membership of both Clubs. The first winner was Alexander Stuart who had the lowest scratch aggregate at the Spring and Autumn Meetings. The score was 176. The same year a Silver Cashmire Cup was

View of the Cathedral grounds, the ruined castle, the town of St Andrews
and the bay, from the top of St Rule's Tower.

Medal Day at St Andrews, 1894, by Messrs Dickenson and Foster of London. The painting, which hangs in the Big Room in the Royal and Ancient Clubhouse, depicts the Rt. Hon. A. J. Balfour driving himself in as Captain of the Club. Tom Morris is seen teeing up for the Captain, and among the other famous personalities in the painting are Willie Auchterlonie, Andrew Lang, Allan Macfie, Horace Hutchinson and Freddie Tait.

Opposite page: Studies of contemporary members of the Royal and Ancient Golf Club (1842), by Charles Lees, R.S.A. *From left to right*: Ferguson Blair of Bathyock, General Moncrieff, Sir John Campbell *(top row)*; Mr Arnot, John Balfour, Dr Gillespie *(middle row)*; Mr Whyte-Melville, an unnamed caddie, Mr Oliphant of Rossie *(bottom row).*

FERGUSON BLAIR of BATHYOCK.

GENL. MONCRIEFF.

SIR JOHN CAMPBELL, BART. OF AIRDS.

MR. ARNOT, ST. ANDREWS.

JOHN BALFOUR ESQ. OF BALBIRNIE.

DR. GILLESPIE, ST. ANDREWS.

MR. WHYTE MELVILLE.

ONE OF THE CADDIES IN MR. LEES' PICTURE.

MR. OLIPHANT OF ROSSIE.

Her Majesty Queen Elizabeth II, Patron of the Royal and Ancient Golf Club, from the portrait by Signor Pietro Annigoni.

View of the wide expanse of fairway of the 1st and 18th holes.

given by the Calcutta Club, the first holder being Major W. B. Craigie from a handicap of 12. At the outset the handicap was based on holes but later changed to strokes, the full difference being given or received. In 1884 Captain D. S. Stewart, the Captain of the Club, gave a trophy in honour of the Queen's Jubilee, which became known as Queen Victoria's Jubilee Vase, played under handicap and the same conditions as the Calcutta Cup, only by singles and decided on the Old Course.

Robert Whyte was the first winner from a handicap of 6. In 1922 the Prince of Wales became Captain of the Club and presented another replica of the Silver Cup to mark a new series of hanging silver balls. The following year the Royal Queensland Golf Club presented a Silver

Boomerang as a prize for the lowest net handicap score at the Autumn Meeting. Lord Airedale was the first winner with a return of 72.

It is tempting to list other landmarks in the Club's history, but the choice is wide. In 1851 it was decided that a railway line would be laid alongside the links. In 1865 Tom Morris was appointed the first professional of the Royal and Ancient. In 1867 the first Ladies' Club was formed at St Andrews. One hundred and ten years later the Ladies' Golf Union moved their headquarters to St Andrews. In 1888 the Royal and Ancient issued Rules of Golf to all golf clubs, and in 1897 was given sole control of the Rules of Golf Committee. In 1919 it assumed the management of British Championships. In 1922 the Prince of Wales played as Captain of the Royal and Ancient. In 1929 the R. and A. legalised steel shafts in Great Britain. In 1933 spectators were charged gate money for the first time. Thirteen years later free golf at St Andrews ended. In 1951 a four-day Conference was held between Great Britain, the Dominions and the United States. The Rules were unified and the stymie abolished. Francis Ouimet became the first American Captain of the R. and A. Twenty-four years later Joseph C. Dey became the second American to hold this office. Television history was made in 1955 when for the first time the Open Championship and the Walker Cup match were televised live from the Old Course. In 1959 the first Ladies' Commonwealth Team Tournament was held on the Old Course, the following year marked the Centenary Open Championship, then in 1970 Sunday practice was allowed for the first time. Another blow to the purists was the installation of fairway watering on the Old Course in 1978. Bringing comfort up to date in St Andrews, the Old Course Golf and Country Club was formally opened by Princess Anne in 1983.

Of all innovations and so-called improvements the one that upset most people was the installation of traffic lights on the first and eighteenth fairways!

Right:
King George VI who as Duke of York was Captain of the Royal and Ancient Golf Club in 1930.

CHAPTER 3
THE OLD COURSE HOLE BY HOLE

CHAPTER 3
THE OLD COURSE HOLE BY HOLE

CHARLES B. MACDONALD, the controversial, brilliant golf course architect, became obsessed with the dream of designing a course which embodied the features of the finest holes in the game. The National Golf Links of America owes its existence to this imaginative idea. Tom Simpson, the doyen of golf course architecture, was our answer to Macdonald. His views were equally controversial and at times reactionary, but both were in agreement that the classic concept of design was based on the principles embodied in the greatest of classics, the Old Course at St Andrews.

This view may be too restrictive for some, yet few would contradict Simpson's assertion that 'the vital thing about a hole is that it should either be more difficult than it looks or look more difficult than it is. It must never be what it looks'. These words certainly apply to the Old Course. As a connoisseur of golfing excellence, Simpson used to argue that a bunker should never be sited to trap a bad shot. If the course had been laid out properly, the mistake would find its own punishment, but at St Andrews the credit cannot be entirely claimed by golf architects. In a very real sense, Nature created the course. It evolved in its own way. There is no suggestion in the lay-out of the neat-looking, well-groomed, orthodox designs of current architecture. The Old Course was shaped by natural forces such as moulded links like Westward Ho, Aberdovey, Machrihanish and Harlech.

The process began when the sea receded, leaving sand-banks and channels of salt water that slowly dried out. In time these ridges became wind-scarred sand-dunes of marram while the sheltered valleys were carpeted with bent and fescue that in turn attracted colonies of rabbits, the right ingredients to anticipate a links of excellent golfing turf. Just when that happened is difficult to say. As far as St Andrews is concerned, the earliest mention of golf is in a parchment housed in the University Library. It is a licence dated 25 January 1552, granted by John Hamilton 'by the mercie of God archebischop of Sanctandros, primat and Legat natie of the haill realme of Scotland' to the inhabitants of the city in return for permission to plant and plenish 'cuniggis' (rabbits) within the north part of their common Links next adjacent to the water of Eden, covenants within the City to accept the community's right 'inter alia to play at golf, futball, schuting, at all gamis with all uther maner of pastime, as ever thai pleis', not only where the 'cuniggis' were plenished but in other parts of the links, and 'in ony tyme cuming'.

Golf was clearly played before that date for this Grant was confirmation of rights previously established by usage. An earlier reference to the game in Scotland occurred when James II decreed in 1457 that 'the futball and the golfe be utterly cripit downe and not usit, and at the bowe merkis be mude at ilke proch Kirk a pair of

butts, and schiting be usit ilk Sunday. And as tuichande the futball and the golfe we ordane it to be punyst be the baronye unlawe.'

A primitive lay-out was in existence before the University was founded in 1413. The number of holes varied over the years. The original links at Leith and Blackheath had five holes, later extended to seven like North Berwick and the London Scottish Volunteers on Wimbledon Common. St Andrews settled for twelve which eventually became twenty-two. The problem was the narrowness of the strip of land available. Being less than forty yards wide, it ruled out separate holes for going out and coming home. Golfers played eleven holes out to the turn by the Eden estuary and returned using the same fairways and greens. The twenty-two-hole course began near the Martyrs' Monument. In 1764, the Royal and Ancient Club passed a resolution that the first four holes should be converted into two, a change that reduced the round to eighteen. Eventually six of the nine greens were extended laterally to allow two holes to be cut upon them, making possible the enormous double greens for which the Old Course is famous. A new site for the seventeenth green was chosen. When the eighteen separate holes were first played, the original nine holes were used on the outward half and the six holes on the extended greens with the new seventeenth green on the return journey. By 1842, the general lay-out of the links was as today. The outline of the course has not changed. Up to World War I there were right-hand and left-hand courses used alternately a week at a time. By accident, the 1886 Amateur Championship, won by Horace Hutchinson, was played on the left-hand course. According to the rota, it should have been used. The Championship was under way before the officials realised what had happened. It was completed over the left-hand course for the first and last time.

The original nine holes all had names and are recorded in a set of verses *The Nine Holes of the Links* of St Andrews in Robert Clark's *Golf; A Royal and Ancient Game*, and are interesting not only as a contemporary view of the Old Course before it was widened, but because the writers were men of letters and keen golfers. *R.C.* was Robert Chambers senior, the founder with his brother William of W. & R. Chambers of Edinburgh, *Chambers' Journal*, *The Book of Days*, *Encyclopaedia* and *Dictionary*. A prominent member of the Royal and Ancient Club, he is buried within the Square Tower of St Rule. *R.C.Jr.* was Robert Chambers junior, his son who died at an early age. A good golfer, he won the first Open Amateur Tournament held at St Andrews. *P.P.A.* was Patric Proctor Alexander, a prominent member of the Royal and Ancient Club. He left a number of verses and sonnets on a wide range of subjects. He was also no mean golfer.

Opposite:
The Old Course Golf and Country Club, with the age-old stone bridge over the Swilcan Burn in the foreground.

The First or Bridge Hole
R.C.

Sacred to hope and promise is the spot –
  To Philp's and to the Union Parlour near,
  To every Golfer, every caddie dear –
Where we strike off – oh, ne'er to be forgot,
Although in lands most distant we sojourn.
  But not without its perils is the place;
  Mark the opposing caddie's sly grimace,
Whispering: 'He's on the road!' 'He's in the burn!'
  So is it often in the grander game
    Of life, when, eager, hoping for the palm,
    Breathing of honour, joy, and love and fame,
    Conscious of nothing like a doubt or qualm,
We start, and cry: 'Salute us, muse of fire!'
And the first footstep lands us in the mire.

The Second or Cartgate Hole
R.C.

Fearful to Tyro is thy primal stroke,
  O Cartgate! for behold the bunker opes
  Right to the teeing-place its yawning chops,
Hope to engulf ere it is well awoke,
That passed, a Scylla in the form of rushes
  Nods to Charybdis which in ruts appears:
  He will be safe who in the middle steers;
One step aside, the ball destruction brushes.
Golf symbols thus again our painful life,
  Dangers in front, and potfalls on each hand:
  But see, one glorious cleek-stroke from the sand
Sends Tyro home, and saves all further strife!
He's in at six – Old Sandy views the lad
With new respect, remarking: 'That's no bad.'

The Third Hole
R.C.

No rest in Golf – still perils in the path:
  Here, playing a good ball, perhaps it goes
  Gently into the *Principalian Nose*,
  Or else *Tam's Coo*, which equally is death.
Perhaps the wind will catch it in mid-air,
  And take it to *the Whins* – 'Look out, look out!
  Tom Morris, be, oh be, a faithful scout.'
But Tom, though *links*-eyed, finds not anywhere.
Such thy mishaps, O Merit: feeble balls
  Meanwhile, roll on, and lie upon the green;
'Tis well, my friends, if you, when this befalls,
  Can Spare yourselves the infamy of spleen.
It only shows the ancient proverb's force,
That you may further go and fare the worse.

The Fourth or Ginger-Beer Hole
P.P.A.

Though thou hast lost this last unlucky hole,
  I prythee, friend, betake thee not to swearing,
  Or other form of speech too wildly daring,
Though some allege it tendeth to console.
Rather do thou thy swelling griefs control,
  Sagacious that at hand a joy awaits thee
  (since out of doubt a glass of beer elates thee),
Without that frightful peril to thy soul.
A pot of beer! go dip thine angry beak in it,
  And straight its rage shall melt to soft placidity,
That solace finding thou art wise to seek in it;
Ah! do not thou on that poor plea reject it,
  That in thine inwards it may breed acidity –
One glass of Stewart's brandy will correct it.

The Hell Hole
P.P.A.

What daring genius first did name the *Hell*?
  What high, poetic, awe-struck grand old Golfer?
  Misdeem him not, ye pious ones, a scoffer –
Whoe'er he was, the name befits thee well.
'All hope abandon, ye who enter here'
  Is written awful o'er thy sandy jaws,
  Whose greedy threat may give the boldest pause,
And frequent from within comes tones of fear –
Dread sounds of cleeks, which ever smite in vain
And – for mere mortal patience is but scanty –
Shriekings thereafter as of souls in pain,
  Dire gnashings of the teeth, and horrid curses,
  With which I need not decorate my verses,
Because, in fact, you'll find them all in Dante.

The Heather Hole
P.P.A.

Ah me! prodigious woes do still environ –
  To quote *verbatim* from some grave old poet –
The man who needs must 'meddle with his iron';
  And here, if ever, thou art doomed to know it.
For now behold thee, doubtless for thy sins,
  Tilling some bunker, as if on a lease of it,
  And so, assiduous to make due increase of it;
Or wandering homeless through a world of whins!
And when – these perils past – thou seemest *dead*,
  And hop'st a half – O woe! thy ball runs crooked,
Making thy foe just one more hole ahead,
  Surely a consummation all too sad
Without that sneering devilish 'Niver lookit',
  The closing comment of the opposing cad.

The High or Eden Hole
R.C.Jr.

The shelly pit is cleared at one fell blow,
  A stroke to be remembered in your dreams!
  But here the Eden on your vision gleams,
Lovely, but treach'rous in its solemn flow.
The hole is perched aloft, too near the tide,
  The green is small and broken is the ground
  Which doth that little charmed space surround!
Go not too far, and go not to the side;
Take the short spoon to do your second stroke;
  Sandy entreats you will the wind take heed on,
For, oh, it would a very saint provoke,
  If you should let your ball plump in the Eden.
You do your best, but who can fate control?
So here against you is another hole.

The Short Hole
R.C.Jr.

Brief but not easy is the next adventure;
  Legend avers it has been done in *one*,
  Though such long *steals* are now but rarely done –
In *three* 'twere well that you the hole should enter.
Strangely original is this bit of ground,
  For while at hand the smooth and smiling green,
  One bunker wide and bushy yawns between,
Where Tyro's gutta is too often found.
Nervous your rival strikes and heels the ball –
  From that whin-bush at six he'd scarce extract it;
  Yours, by no blunder this time counteracted,
Is with the grass-club lofted over all.
There goes a hole in your side – how you hug it!
Much as th' Australian digger does a nugget.

The End Hole
R.C.Jr.

The end, but not the end – the distance post
   That halves the game – a serious point to thee,
   For if one more thou losest, twill be *three*:
Yet even in that case, think not all is lost.
Men four behind have been, on the return,
   So favoured by Olympus, or by care,
   That all their terrors vanished into air,
And caddies cried them dormy at the burn!
I could quote proverbs did I speak at random:
   Full many a broken ship comes into port,
   Full many a cause is gained at last resort,
But Golf impresses most, *Nil desperandum*.
Turn, then, my son, with two against, nor dread
To gain the winning-post with one ahead

Turning from the past to the present, it is interesting to analyse the reasons for the reputation of the Old Course as being one of the world's greatest tests of a player. Initial reaction to the course is not always so complimentary; in fact the opinion often expressed is that the reputation has been exaggerated, until gradually a fuller appreciation is felt. Here is an examination of golfing skills in which a fine shot is rewarded. If not, it is punished. Every shot has to be carefully planned. It is impossible to ignore the subtlety of natural bunkers ranging from yawning caverns to hidden pot-bunkers. Fairways can deny a level stance, while the contours of enormous plateau greens have cunning slopes and undulations which put a premium on reading a line and judging pace. It is a contest of strategy often influenced if not resolved by the wind which is the ultimate hazard at St Andrews, particularly when it sweeps from left to right across the fairways of the first, eleventh, sixteenth and seventeenth. Many of the holes of classic quality and design command affection and respect. Together they explain why Bobby Jones once said that if he had to play his golf on only one course, he would without hesitation have chosen the Old Course.

Card of the Course
Hole 1   Burn   370 yards   par 4

The beginning seems innocuous. On the tee the widest fairway in the world stretches out in front of you with no rough and bunker-free. The white rails on the right are out-of-bounds, but anyone so penalised would accept the penalty for such a wild shot. More worrying is the thought that the shot has to be played in front of the windows of the Royal and Ancient Clubhouse, where members are prone to be critical. About 150 yards from the tee the fairway is bisected by Granny Clark's Wynd, which has meaning only to those knowledgeable about St Andrews history.

The second shot is more demanding and can be misleading. Distances can be misjudged. It is longer than it seems and without enough club, the Swilcan Burn is waiting with a penalty shot for lifting and dropping on the side farther from the hole. Doug Sanders was such a victim in the 1970 Open when the hole cost him a six. Fortunately, the area beyond is free of problems. The line to the hole is slightly left and fortune usually favours the bold.

Hole 1   Burn
370 yards   Par 4

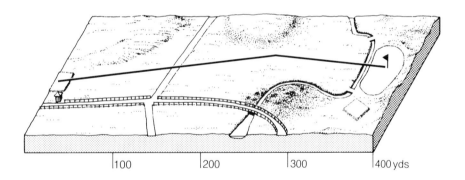

| 100 | 200 | 300 | 400 yds |

After a carefree start, the pressure is on. The fairway
looks horribly narrow with plenty of rough and gorse.
The bunkering is potentially lethal, particularly
Cheape's Bunker and a couple farther on. The line from
the tee is right of Cheape's. Even then a direct shot to the
hole is threatened by a pot bunker centrally placed and
eating into the green. A bold shot will clear it and
perhaps stay on with the likelihood of an enormous putt.
More sensible is to take the right side of the green,
leaving a more manageable putt. So much depends on
the wind. Coming from the north-west, the hole plays
long and needs accurate club selection for the second
shot.

Hole 2   Dyke
411 yards   Par 4

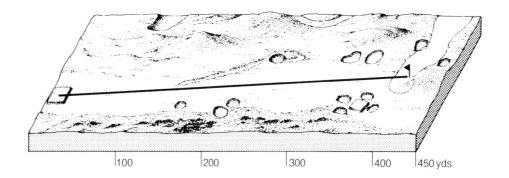

|100 |200 |300 |400 |450 yds

Hole 3   Cartgate (out)   371 yards   par 4

Shares a double green with the fifteenth. The deep Cartgate Bunker on the left side of a green that slopes away is
the main worry, plus three bunkers and the Principal's
Nose. The drive means taking a risk over the rough on
the right side. Once negotiated, the way is clear for a
run-up or pitch to the hole.

Hole 3   Cartgate
352 (371) yards   Par 4

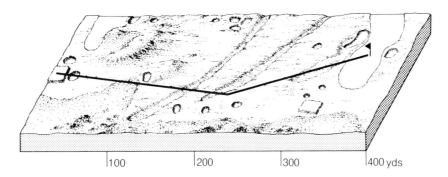

100   200   300   400 yds

39

Hole 4   Ginger Beer   463 yards   par 4

Many regard Ginger Beer as one of the toughest holes. It calls for an accurate drive along a valley between a plateau and a sea of gorse, with bunkers fringing the rough and the green. The Student's Bunker on the left by the green commands respect. A grassy mound in the centre has to be considered. A choice of line is either straight on the pin which can be a venture of faith, or, more cautiously, to drive to the left of the plateau, which gives a clear approach to the pin.

Hole 4   Ginger Beer
419 (463) yards   Par 4

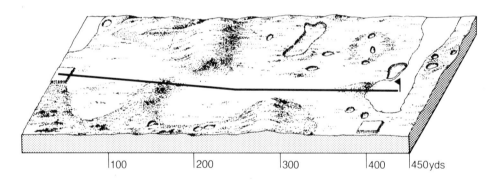

100   200   300   400   450yds

40

The Old Course Golf and Country Club, opened by HRH Princess Anne
in 1983.

Bernhard Langer drives from the short 11th in the 1984 Open Championship.

Aerial view of the Road Hole, the 1st and the 18th holes with the Royal and
Ancient Clubhouse in the background.

The dreaded road hazard at the 17th.

Hole 5   Hole o' Cross (out)   564 yards   par 5

An over-confident drive aimed straight at the distant hole can invite disaster. A gaggle of seven bunkers lurks about 250 yards from the tee, while another couple are sited in the face of a hill short of the green, with a gully beyond. The wiser line is to the left towards the Elysian Fields where a firm second shot could find the plateau green shared with the thirteenth, though possibly a pitch may be needed from the hill in front of the green. The influence of wind on the hole was demonstrated by Craig Wood when, aided by a near-gale-force wind, he drove into the bunkers about 50 yards from the green. Lesser mortals are not so ambitious.

Hole 5   Hole o' Cross
514 (564) yards   Par 5

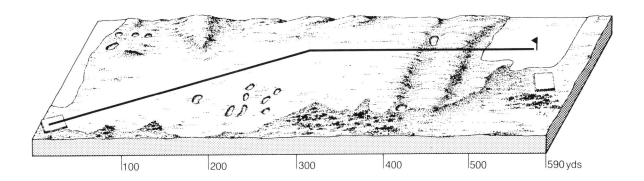

| 100 | 200 | 300 | 400 | 500 | 590 yds |

Hole 6   Heathery (out)   416 yards   par 4

This hole has heather and whins on the right, pot bunkers on the left, with the green protected by a slight ridge that can mislead. Underclubbing the second shot is common. The line is away from the green to the left, leaving a pitch shot to the pin.

Hole 6   Heathery
374 (416) yards   Par 4

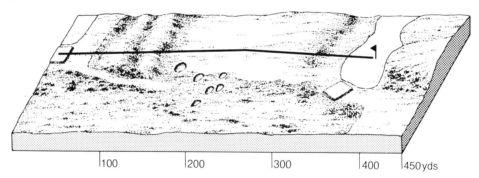

| | 100 | 200 | 300 | 400 | 450 yds |

Hole 7   High (out)   372 yards   par 4

This hole, dog-legged to the right, marks the beginning
of the Loop that produces some remarkably low scoring.
It calls for an accurate tee-shot avoiding whins on the
right and the Cockle Bunker guarding the high plateau
green shared with the eleventh. The puzzling slopes are
tricky to read.

Hole 7   High
359 (372) yards   Par 4

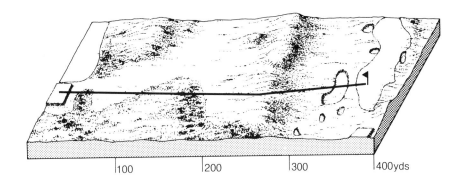

|100 |200 |300 |400yds

Hole 8   Short   178 yards   par 3

Not an exacting short hole. A useful drive should avoid
the ridge and the small but deep bunker in the face of the
green which falls away.

Hole 8   Short
178 yards   Par 3

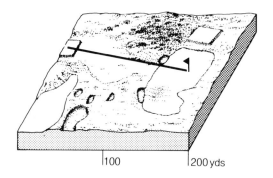

100   200 yds

Hole 9   End   356 yards   par 4

Two bunkers are prominent. Kruger about 100 yards from the tee is in the direct line; Mrs Kruger is in the heather on the left. Two smaller traps have to be avoided. Boase's and the End Hole are on the right with a third guarding the left-hand corner of the green. Should be a straightforward par.

Out 3,501 yards: par 36

Hole 9   End
307 (356) yards   Par 4

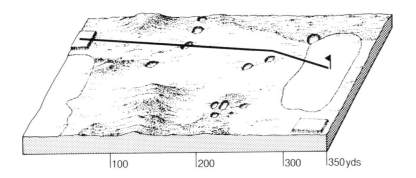

100   200   300   350 yds

Hole 10   Bobby Jones   342 yards   par 4

Another hole which should not create undue problems. The bunker about 100 yards from the tee is not a worry and only a slice would find the trap on the right. The green is free of bunkers but falls away to the right. The hole was named in 1972 as a tribute to the famous American golfer.

Hole 10   Bobby Jones
318 (342) yards   Par 4

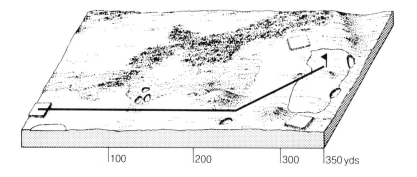

100   200   300   350 yds

Hole 11   High (in)   172 yards   par 3

This par 3 is one of the most copied holes in golf and has exercised significant influence on strategic design. Charles Blair Macdonald, America's first accepted golf architect, not only incorporated a replica in the National Golf Links on Long Island, but included similar versions in his other lay-outs. Alister Mackenzie, the Scottish-born doctor who emigrated to the United States and abandoned medicine for golf, was influenced by Bobby Jones's admiration for the High and adopted a free-style version at Augusta with individualistic differences. In Augusta the Strath Bunker protects the centre of the green, Hill Bunker is not so penal, the green is a different design, and the length is longer, but the strategy is on a par with the original.

Strath is the key hazard. This deep, steep bunker eats into the front right-hand edge of the green. If the ball finishes against the wall, even an explosion shot can fail to make the putting surface. A sliced shot is the likeliest victim, while a pulled shot is earmarked for the ten-foot-deep Hill Bunker. It may not be so punishing as Strath, but is an unforgiving trap. They are the golfing equivalent of Scylla and Charybdis. Assuming these bunkers have been avoided, troubles are by no means over. If the ball finished above the hole, the slope from back to front is at such a steep angle that putting is fiendishly difficult. An overstrong tee-shot will finish in the rough by the back of the Eden. When that happens, if a strong wind blows down the slope, the odds are that the downhill putt will finish off the grass into Strath.

The eleventh justifies its reputation as one of the greatest short holes in the world.

Hole 11   High
172 yards   Par 3

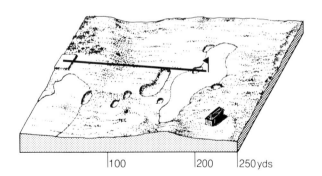

|100 |200 |250 yds

Hole 12   Heathery (in)   316 yards   par 4

A deceptive hole that snares a player into trouble. From tee to green there seems nothing to worry about, perfectly safe to belt the ball down the fairway. Closer acquaintance shows it to be infested with concealed bunkers. The architect is not to blame for such deception. This was the original High Hole reversed. Played in the opposite direction, the bunkers are clearly visible. Now, half-a-dozen traps lurk on the reverse sides of the undulations. Local knowledge gained the hard way is the only answer. Even then, it is a relief to reach the narrow plateau green, either by an accurate drive to the right followed by a tight run-up, or out to the left by the heather-covered hill and a crisp pitch to clear a bunker.

Hole 12   Heathery
316 yards   Par 4

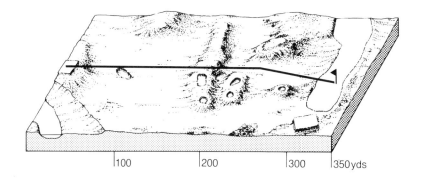

|100 |200 |300 |350yds

Hole 13   Hole o'Cross (in)   425 yards   par 4

The names of the bunkers guarding this first-class hole, with its enormous green on a plateau, are part of the Old Course history. Those caught in the traps are hardly appreciative of such significance, but all are bound up with the past. The Coffin Bunkers are sited to catch a fairly long drive. A more hesitant shot can finish in Nick's Bunker. The Cat's Trap Bunker and Walkinshaw's are waiting ahead of Coffins. Close to the green is the Lions's Mouth pot bunker, with the Hole o'Cross Bunker at the back of the green. The drive should be steered out to the left by the sixth fairway which will open up the green.

Hole 13   Hole o'Cross
398 (425) yards   Par 4

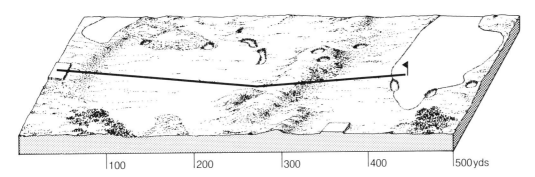

100   200   300   400   500 yds

49

Hole 14   Long   567 yards   par 5

This longest hole of the round, a true par five, is a classic that can be tackled by alternative routes. Tactics are dictated by the wind. Every change of direction means fresh problems. The broad strategy is clear. The drive has to avoid the out-of-bounds on the right and the Beardies, those five pot bunkers hiding in the tough rough before reaching the Elysian Fields. It is a temporary respite before deciding how to tackle the yawning Hell Bunker immediately ahead. Given a favourable wind, it is tempting to go for the carry, but behind lie the Ginger Beer bunker and the Grave. The option of taking either a left-hand or right-hand line will leave a difficult shot to the tilting green. Those who play safe are more than thankful to get a par if the wind is right, otherwise the odds are against. Survival is often all that matters, as innumerable famous players have found when scores of seven or more have ruined many a championship chance. Bobby Locke saw his Open title founder in the Beardies and Hell; the latter cost Gene Sarazen eight shots and the Championship. Peter Thomson collected a seven in the Beardies and the Grave, but managed to recover to win. The undoubted greatness of this hole lies in its never-ending problems. It is a stern examination of a player's skill and courage.

Hole 14   Long
523 (567) yards   Par 5

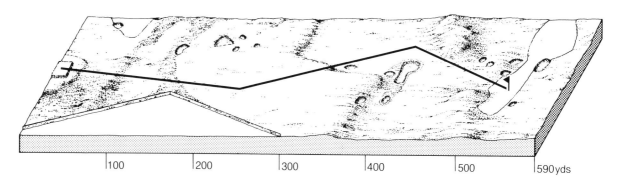

100   200   300   400   500   590yds

Hole 15   Cartgate (in)   413 yards   par 4

Another hole where strategically sited bunkers dictate tactics. The best line is to skirt Cottage Bunker and avoid the Sutherland pot bunker further on which would open up the green from the gully. Accurate club selection is vital.

Hole 15   Cartgate
401 (413) yards   Par 4

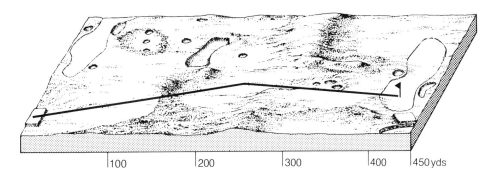

100   200   300   400   450 yds

The direction of the wind and the Principal's Nose Bunker hold the key to this classic hole. With the wind behind or on a calm day, it should be possible to carry the Principal's Nose, though there is always the danger of ending up in Deacon Sime ahead. Against the wind, it is another story. A decision has to be taken whether to choose the line to the right or left of the Principal's Nose. Possibly the safer is the left route where the fairway is open, but the shot must be gauged accurately, otherwise Wig Bunker and Grant's Bunker are pitfalls. The alternative demands a tight drive down a narrow thirty-yard gap between the Principal's Nose and out-of-bounds. The reward for taking the risk successfully is a simple pitch or pitch-and-run to the terraced green. Immense satisfaction when everything comes off.

Hole 16   Corner of the Dyke
351 (382) yards   Par 4

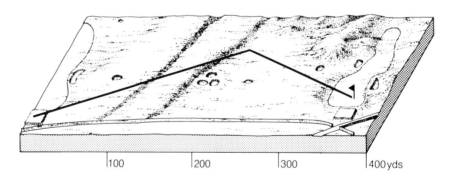

|100 |200 |300 |400 yds

Hole 17   Road   461 yards   par 4

Probably the best-known hole in the world, certainly the most feared. For years it has taken a toll of would-be champions. The drive is over the railway sheds, now restored, avoiding the out-of-bounds wall of the Old Course Hotel, taking a line down the right side of the fairway to open up the narrow plateau green. The iron shot has to be steered away from the bunker, probably deliberately short, so as to round off with a chip and a putt. Either route is perilous.

The notorious Road Bunker is an awesome trap eating into the heart of the narrow plateau green, while beyond, running diagonally, is the dreaded road and a stone wall. Only the most confident play for the top level of the green. An overhit means disaster. Too timid and the ball trickles into the Road Bunker. Other hazards include Cheape's Bunker, Scholar's Bunker and Progressing Bunker, but the hazards that intimidate are the Road Bunker and the road itself. The Japanese professional, Tsuneyuki Nakajima found that to his cost in the 1978 Open when he needed four shots to get out of the Road Bunker and a nine went on his card. Nerves of steel are needed at this notorious hole. Relaxing is out of the question.

Hole 17   Road
461 yards   Par 4

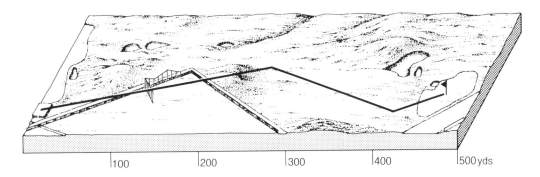

100   200   300   400   500 yds

After the trauma of the Road Hole, the eighteenth is almost an anti-climax, but it would be a mistake to take it for granted. Admittedly, there is no worry about the Swilcan Burn, and the complete absence of bunkers is a relief. To finish on the surface of Granny Clark's Wynd might pose a slight problem for there is no free drop and the shot has to be played from where the ball lies. The danger is being short and coming to rest in the smooth hollow of the Valley of Sin. The slope is more pro-

nounced than it looks and timid shots have a habit of rolling back. An overstrong pitch-and-run can also be costly. Downhill from the back of the huge green often requires three putts, as Doug Sanders discovered.

In 3,432 yards: par 36
Total 6,933 yards: par 72

Hole 18   Tom Morris
354 yards   Par 4

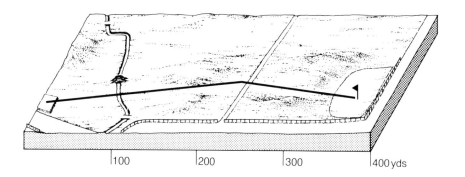

100   200   300   400 yds

Fulsome praise without confirmation is mere rhetoric, but in the case of the Old Course most of the world's greatest golfers have paid their tributes over the years. Apart from the likes of Bobby Jones and Gene Sarazen, the South African, Bobby Locke, admitted that the proudest moment of his life was winning the Open Championship on the Old Course; Peter Thomson named it the best course in the world; Jack Nicklaus, after winning the 1970 Open, declared that he would rather win a championship at St Andrews than anywhere else in the world. The former United States Open Champion, Ed Furgol, was not so complimentary on his introduction to the Old Course. His views might have been slightly jaundiced after the fourteenth had cost him successive sevens, but the current opinion was expressed by Tom Watson in an interview published in *Golf World* when he said, 'St Andrews is the first course you think of when you think of championship golf. It is the birthplace of the game. Playing there is a very special experience. Winning there would carry very special meaning for me. The course is virtually everything modern architecture is not. All architects should make a pilgrimage to St Andrews. We've taken the concept of target golf way too literally. The first thing that struck me when I played there in 1978, when I was tied for the lead going into the last round and finished in a tie for fourteenth, was the comparative ease of the first and eighteenth holes. Gene Sarazen likes that. He thinks the critical hole should be half-way through the second nine, rather than have everything boil down to the closing hole. Then there are the double greens, the bunkers with their historic names. . . . It's a memorable, memorable place.'

The Old Course is a precious possession and it is right only at St Andrews, the ultimate golfing test of courage and skill.

CHAPTER 4
THE ERA OF ALLAN ROBERTSON

CHAPTER 4
THE ERA OF ALLAN ROBERTSON

ALLAN ROBERTSON WAS the first professional golfer of note and best known member of one of the oldest golfing families in St Andrews. Contemporary accounts give a fairly detailed pen portrait of this interesting man against an early golfing background, though some err on the side of flowery exaggerations. One of the worst offenders was the Reverend J. G. McPherson, who wrote *Golf and Golfers Past and Present* in 1891 from a country manse, and named Allan Robertson as the greatest golfer of all time. A more restrained description came from the pen of James Balfour, who in 1887 produced a small paper-clad book of memories titled *Reminiscences of Golf on St Andrews Links* which sold for one shilling. No mean player himself, being a Medallist of the Royal and Ancient and father of Leslie Balfour-Melville, his description of Robertson makes an acceptable word-picture: 'Allan Robertson and his father and grandfather had been ball-makers, when feather balls were the only balls, for more than a hundred years. He was a short, little, active man, with a pleasant face, small features, and a merry twinkle in his eye. He was universally popular, not a bit forward, but withal easy and full of self-respect. He generally wore a red, round jacket, and played constantly with gentlemen, both in matches of great importance, and in those that were only more or less important. His style was neat and effective. He held his clubs near the end of the handle, even his putter high up. His clubs were light, and his stroke an easy, swift switch. With him the game was one as much of head as of hand. He always kept cool and generally pulled through a match even when he was behind. He was a natural gentleman, honourable and true. He died of jaundice on 1st September 1859, when only about the age of forty-four, much regretted.'

The reputation of the Robertson family as golf ball makers is confirmed in earlier sources. Mathieson's poem of *The Goff*, published in 1743, a copy of which was sold at auction in 1985 for a five-figure sum, anticipates a match:

Two balls with careful eye,
That with *Clarinda's* breasts for colour vye,
The work of *Bobson* who, with matchless art,
Shapes the firm hide, connecting every part,
Then in a socket sets the well-stitch'd void
And thro' the eyelet drives the downy tide;
Crowds urging crowds the forceful brogue impels,
The feathers harden and the leather swells;
He crams and sweats, yet crams and urges more
Till scarce the turgid globe contains its store. . . .

Soon as *Hyperion* gilds old *Andrea's* spires
From bed the artist to his cell retires;
With bended back, there plies his steely awls,
And shapes and stuffs and finishes the balls.

The short, stocky, bewhiskered Allan Robertson, who died in 1859, was described by W.W. Tulloch as 'the most interesting personality in golf in the first half of the nineteenth century'.

It is accepted that Bobson who lived by Andrea's spires was a Robertson who lived at St Andrews. A century later the Robertson skill as a ball-maker is still established and is confirmed by George Fullerton Carnegie, an Angus laird who was born at Pitarrow in 1800 and published in 1833 for private circulation a poem *Golfiana* in which he described St Andrews and its characters of his day. Peter Robertson died in 1803. His son, David, is referred to in Carnegie's poem:

> Great Davie Robertson, the eldest cad,
> In whom the good was stronger than the bad;
> He sleeps in death! and with him sleeps a skill
> Which Davie, statesmanlike, would wield at will!
> Sound be his slumbers! yet if he should wake
> In worlds where golf is play'd, himself he'd stake
> And look about and tell each young beginner,
> 'I'll gie half-ane – nae mair, as I'm a sinner.'
> He leaves a son, and Allan is his name.
> In golfing far beyond his father's fame.

David Robertson was in demand as a player and a teacher, yet his status was that of a senior caddie, 'the oldest of the cads', for the term *professional* was still unknown. Davie was the last of the senior caddies, while Allan was the first of the professionals, with a rare skill as a ball-maker.

In less poetic terms, the art of ball making was uniform up to 1848. They were made of leather stuffed with feathers until they were just as hard as a rackets ball. The leather, softened with water and alum, was cut in three sections and sewn together with waxed thread. The feathers were stuffed through a hole with a blunt-pointed stuffing-iron that was fixed to the maker's shoulder with an arm-type crutch. The finished ball weighed about 26–30 drams avoirdupois and measured roughly an inch and a quarter in diameter. Once dried, they were given three coats of white oil paint to offset the effect of water. The average production rate was between five and ten balls a day. St Andrews was a recognised manufacturing centre with a steady demand, because every round required about half-a-dozen balls. They were not cheap. Robertson charged 1s 8d a ball, which was cheaper than the two shillings for one produced by Gourlay of Musselburgh. It was not all St Andrews consumption. Sales to places like Edinburgh, Aberdeen, Glasgow and Perth topped 10,000 balls a year. Of these the Robertsons' product was regarded as the best. He was the leading ball-maker of St Andrews. He was assisted by Tom Morris, who was six years younger, and 'Lang Willie', a very tall caddie, about six feet two, a familiar figure in early prints with bent knees and slouching gait, a tall hat, swallow-tailed blue coat and light trousers. The three men used Robertson's kitchen as a workshop. The balls were sold through a window on the corner of Links Place. Their production rate is chronicled. In 1840 a total of 1,021 feather-balls were made; in 1841 the total had increased to 1,390; in 1844 it was 2,455 balls.

All that changed with the appearance of the gutta-percha balls. Various suggestions have been made as to how it was conceived, but the most probable comes from a former Secretary to the University of St Andrews, Andrew Bennett, who recorded in *The St Andrews Golf Club Centenary, 1843–1943*, that 'it is believed that the idea of using gutta-percha for golf balls originated with one Paterson, a Medical Missioner in Burma, whose brother, living in Lauder, set about making balls with the material sent from the East, and sent specimens to Edinburgh, Blackheath and London about 1848. The gutta-percha reached this country in strips used for the wrapping of a Burmese idol presented as a curio to St Andrews University, his Alma Mater, by the Burmese Minister.'

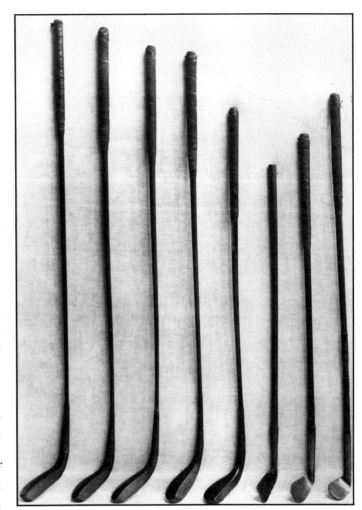

A selection of eighteenth and nineteenth century clubs. *From left to right:* driver, by William Dunn the elder; brassey (1850); long spoon; short spoon (1850); putter; sand iron (1770); sand iron (1800); track iron (1881).

61

Their first use by members of the Royal and Ancient Golf Club was described by James Balfour: 'About the beginning of the year 1848 balls were first made of gutta-percha. I remember the commencement of them perfectly. My brother-in-law, Admiral Maitland Dougall, played a double match at Blackheath with the late Sir Ralph Anstruther and William Adam of Blair-Adam and another friend with gutta-percha balls on a very wet day. They afterwards dined together at Sir Charles Adam's at Greenwich Hospital, and Sir Charles said after dinner: "A most curious thing – here is a golf ball of gutta percha; Maitland and I have played with it all day in the rain, and it flies better at the end of the day than it did at the beginning." Maitland came to Edinburgh immediately after and told me of this. We at once wrote to London for some of these balls, and went to Musselburgh to try them. Gourlay the ball-maker had heard of them, and followed us round. He was astonished to see how they flew, and, being round, how they rolled straight to the hole on the putting-green. He was alarmed for his craft, and having an order from Sir David Baird to send him some balls whenever he had a supply by him, he forwarded to him that evening six dozen! Sir David accordingly was one of the last who adhered to the feather balls, and did not acknowledge the superiority of the others until his large supply had finished.

'At first they were made with the hand by rolling them on a flat board; thus made, they were round and smooth. They were not painted, but used with their natural brown colour. When new, they did not fly well, but ducked in the air. To remedy this they were hammered with a heavy hammer, but this did not effect the object. They still ducked until they got some rough usage from the cleek or iron. This made cuts on their sides, which were not liked; but it made them fly. These cuts were easily removed by dipping them in hot water at night, but it spoiled the ball. About this time it occurred to an ingenious saddler in South Street to hammer them all round with the thin or sharp end of the hammer. The experiment was completely successful, and the ball thus hammered came rapidly into use, and they were soon improved by being painted.

'But the ball-makers were still bitterly opposed to them, as they threatened to destroy their trade, and both Allan and Tom resolved that they would never play in a match where these balls were used. In an unlucky hour, however, Tom good-naturedly broke his pledge, and played with a gentleman as his partner who had gutta balls. When Allan discovered it he was much annoyed with Tom. Tom, when he saw this, gave up his employment under him, and opened a shop of his own, where he made both kinds of balls, and also clubs.'

Not long afterwards Allan Robertson changed his mind. Instead of bribing caddies to give him all the gutties they could find so that he could burn them, he realised the new ball need not ruin his trade. The number of new players increased; in the past many had been deterred by the short life of the expensive balls. Moreover, Robertson anticipated the need for a new type of iron club. The feathery ball jumped off the face of a wooden putter, while the rounded shape of the gutta called for a rolling shot instead of the former stroke. As a result, Robertson introduced a putting cleek for the greens. It revolutionised the short game with irons and had a significant effect on the club-making industry.

Allan Robertson bridged the gap between the feathery and the gutta percha eras and then joined the ranks of those St Andrews craftsmen who instead of producing crude bludgeons created examples of elegant golf clubs in beech, apple, pear and other indigenous hard woods. Among them were James Pett, who made clubs and balls for the Marquis of Montrose in 1672; Robert Wilson of North Street; Henry Mill, supplier of clubs to the University at the beginning of the 18th

The unusual tombstone of Allan Robertson with *right*, detail showing Robertson's face.

century; Tom Stewart in Argyle Street and Condie of Market Street; David Dick of College Wynd, who died in 1731; White, the first blacksmith to concentrate on cleek-making from premises near the Cathedral Pends; James Wilson, one of Hugh Philp's men, who opened his own premises in 1845 on a site now occupied by Rusacks Hotel; but, apart from the McEwans of Musselburgh, none could equal the quality of Hugh Philp's work. This one-time joiner and house painter was appointed clubmaker to the Society of Golfers of St Andrews in September 1819 and moved his works from Argyle Street to a shop by the Union Parlour that served as clubrooms for their members, later transferring to the house that eventually became Tom Morris's shop. On his death in 1856, Philp was succeeded by Robert Forgan.

Much was written about Allan Robertson as a player. The claims are far from modest, and may be exaggerated, but he was unquestionably a fine golfer. He was the first man to break 80 on the Old Course. His 79 was carded in a match against Bethune of Blebo on 15 September 1858. His card read:

Out: – 4–4–4–5–5–6–4–4–4 – 40
In: – 4–3–5–6–4–5–5–4–3 – 39 – 79

Robertson also took part in a series of challenge matches, outstanding being the biggest stake-money clash of the nineteenth century. Four hundred pounds was wagered in 1849 when Robertson and Tom Morris took on the Dunns of Musselburgh. The match was over three greens – Musselburgh, St Andrews and North Berwick in that sequence. Musselburgh saw the Dunns victorious by the huge margin of 13 and 12. St Andrews evened the score after a close fight, and the Robertson/Morris partnership went on to win the decider and the series by an aggregate of two holes.

Allan Robertson never held the position of Club Professional, in fact his name is mentioned only twice in the Royal and Ancient Minutes. The first time was in October, 1856, when the Green Committee was authorised 'to expend the sum of £25 in placing the putting greens into better order, under the superintendence of Allan Robertson.' The only other entry was on 28 September 1859, when the following resolution was entered: 'That this Meeting have heard with deep regret of the death of Allan Robertson and they desire to record in their Minutes the opinion universally entertained of the almost unrivalled skill with which he played the Game of Golf combining a ready and correct judgment with most accurate execution. They desire also to express their sense of the propriety of his whole conduct and unvarying civility with which he mingled with all classes of Golfers, of his cordiality to those of his own, of his integrity, his happy temper and the anxiety which he always manifested to promote the comfort of all who frequented the Links. They desire an extract of this Minute to be transmitted to his widow with an expression of their sympathy in her affliction.' To this might be added as a postscript the words of the Reverend W. W. Tulloch . . . 'Allan Robertson was the most outstanding figure and the most interesting personality on any links in the first half of the nineteenth century.'

CHAPTER 5
TOM MORRIS AND HIS FAMOUS SON

CHAPTER 5
TOM MORRIS AND HIS FAMOUS SON

THE CAREERS OF Tom Morris and his famous son form, in their uncomplicated way, a commentary on the St Andrews of a long-past era. He was the arch over which the game advanced out of a dim past into the twentieth century. Sometimes the legendary figure looms so large that the man himself is lost. It was not the case with Morris. He was an outstanding personality years before newspapers made all men indistinguishable, with a life span so long he outlived most of his contemporaries. When visits to the Old Course became fewer, the public took him more and more to their hearts, a Grand Old Man ready for his *nunc dimittis*, but refusing to speed the departure. He enjoyed life to the full, and there was nowhere in the world like St Andrews.

He was born on 16 June 1821 in North Street. His father, John Morris, a St Andrews man, was employed as a letter-carrier. His mother, Jean Bruce, came from Anstruther. He grew up in an atmosphere of golf, and began to play with a rough-carved miniature club when he was six. The Old Course in the background was remote from the outside world, which today seems like a time-capsule. George IV was on the throne, Napoleon Bonaparte died that year on St Helena, James Monroe was President of the United States and Alexander I was Emperor of Russia. The first steamboat had just crossed the Atlantic, but the Liverpool–Manchester Railway had yet to be opened. It was a world enriched by such men as Wordsworth, Beethoven, Sir Walter Scott, Charles Lamb and Sir Robert Peel. John Keats had just died. Tom Cribb was Champion of England after an epic bare-knuckle fight. Gustavus, a 'shabby little grey' bought for 25 guineas at Hampton Court won the Derby and a prize of £1,758.15s, while John Willes had been 'no-balled' for using round-arm bowling. Such was the world into which Tom Morris was born, and similar topics were discussed when he was a pupil at Madras College. They were, however, too remote to affect everyday life. In Tom's case, golf was to be his job. At the age of eighteen, he was apprenticed to Allan Robertson in the ball-making trade. The association worked well until Morris played in a match in which a gutta-percha ball was used. Robertson, fearful of the effect this new ball could have on the feathery-ball trade, had forbidden its use by anyone who worked for him. There was a row and Morris left to set up a similar business of his own.

In 1851, Colonel Fairlie invited Morris to take a job at Prestwick that would involve looking after the Links. The prospects looked good. It was accepted and lasted for fourteen years. During that time golfing history was made. The Prestwick Club inaugurated an Open tournament in 1860 with a Championship Belt as the prize. Willie Park won the first event. Morris took the next two and repeated the success in 1864 and 1867. In his prime, Tom Morris must have been a fine striker of the ball. He competed in every Open Championship up to and including 1896, the year that Harry Vardon won his first title.

Major Boothby was anxious to tempt Morris back to St Andrews. He proposed at a General Meeting of the Royal and Ancient Club that a first-class professional should be employed as a servant of the Club to take entire charge of the golf course. The suggestion was approved. A salary of £50 a year was fixed, the appointment to be under the control of the Green Committee. On 9 January 1865, Tom Morris attended a full meeting of members in the Clubhouse. The duties were spelt out, and he could employ a man to do the heavy work like carting for two days a week. Upon accepting the post, Morris was formally handed the tools of the job – a barrow, a spade and a shovel.

For the next 44 years Morris spent his life in St Andrews, gaining a reputation that was respected throughout the golfing world. In June 1903 he resigned as greenkeeper, but was made Honorary Greenkeeper with the assurance that his salary of £50 per annum would be continued for the rest of his life. Further tangible recognition was the collection of over £1,000 and the purchase of an annuity of £80 a year, the remainder being invested under trustees. Sir George Reid, President of the Royal Scottish Academy, was commissioned by Royal and Ancient members to paint Morris's picture. The finished portrait hangs in the Club and was first exhibited in August 1903. In his eighty-seventh year Morris had a fall in the New Club and never fully recovered. He died in May 1908. On the day of the funeral there was no play on the Links. It was an imaginative gesture. Tom Morris was, and his memory still is, a symbol of St Andrews.

Tom Morris had his tragedies, like the rest of mankind, but one that hit him hard was the death of his son.

Young Tom was born at Prestwick in 1851. He took to golf as naturally as his father had done and made his first public appearance at a tournament in Perth when he was only 13 years of age. Considered too young to compete in the main event, he was matched against Master William Greig, who was described as a juvenile golfing celebrity. A contemporary report tells all: 'The most interesting match of the day was between Master Morris, son of the redoubtable Tom, and Master Greig of Perth. The latter played with astonishing neatness and precision, but the honours of the day were in store for his competitor. Master Morris seems to have been born and bred to golf. He has been cast in the very mould of a golfer and plays with all the steadiness and certainty, in embryo, of his father. It was funny to see the boys followed by hundreds of deeply interested and anxious spectators.' The reporter was quick to spot a future champion.

In 1867 Young Tom came of age in a golfing sense, for, although he was only sixteen, he tied for first place with Willie Park and Bob Andrews in a tournament at Carnoustie which attracted all the top professionals. Young Tom won the play-off by two shots from Andrews with a card of 132. Park trailed well behind. Bob Andrews was to Perth what Tom Morris was to St Andrews. Born in 1835, he was known as The Rook, and played many matches against the Morrises, father and son. In one of them against Morris senior at Prestwick, he holed out in two to win the match by a fluke. His drive, with the club known as the Black Doctor, was too strong, scattered the crowds round the green, struck a

Lord Balfour driving off as Captain of the Royal and Ancient Golf Club in 1874. His partner, Graham Murray, is on the right whilst Old Tom Morris applauds in the background.

top hat and rebounded onto the green to within inches of the hole.

In 1867 Young Tom made his debut in the Open Championship. He finished fourth behind his father, who won the Belt and £8 prize-money. The following year Young Tom made no mistake. He won the Belt with 154 and a margin of 11 strokes, and repeated the feat in 1869 with 157 and the same margin. He made the Championship Belt his own property in 1870 with a third consecutive win, this by 12 strokes with a total of 149. Prestwick in those days was a 12-hole course and the Championship was decided over three rounds with par for the course being 49. The margins of these three wins emphasises Young Tom's superiority over his contemporaries. The third victory showed an average of 74½ per round and was unbeaten in the Championship as long as the guttie ball was used and the entries included such men as J. H. Taylor, Harry Vardon and James Braid. It was only beaten 34 years later by Jack White at Sandwich.

After Young Tom made the Champion Belt his own property at the age of 19, the Open Championship itself was reviewed. After an interregnum of one year, no Championship being held in 1871, a Silver Cup was presented by the Royal and Ancient Golf Club, Prestwick Golf Club and the Honourable Company of Edinburgh Golfers as a permanent trophy, the winner to receive a Gold Medal. The Championship was to be played at Prestwick, St Andrews and Musselburgh in rotation, the three clubs sharing management of the event. Prestwick staged the 1872 Open and once again Young Tom won, in bad weather, with an aggregate seventeen strokes higher than in 1870.

Without doubt he was the finest golfer of his time. As regards technique, it is difficult to get a clear picture. Photographs are scarce, but contemporary comments suggest a swing that was not as full as the traditional sweeping St Andrews style, nor as rhythmic as Davie Strath's. In spite of pronounced muscular shoulders, he lacked length but compensated with a body action so forceful that at times shafts were broken. This forcing thrust helped in recovery shots from bad lies. His iron shots were outstanding. He introduced the niblick, later the mashie or five-iron, for approach shots. Its value had been demonstrated by Allan Robertson, and Young Tom used it to good effect in a series of matches against Arthur Molesworth, the Westward Ho amateur. On a frostbound course with a small area of each green cleared of snow, Young Tom continually pitched the ball up to the pin knowing that the backspin would make it stop. He played these shots with an open stance rather than with the ball nearer the left foot. On the greens he had an upright stance, used a wooden putter and played the ball almost off the right toe with the left toe pointing at the hole. No weakness was apparent in any of his shot-making.

Everything pointed to a long, outstanding career, when his life changed overnight. He was playing with his father in a challenge match at North Berwick against the brothers, Willie and Mungo Park, when a telegram was delivered to the clubhouse. It said that Young Tom's wife was dangerously ill. Provost Brodie decided not to hand it over until the match ended. A yacht belonging to John Lewis, an Edinburgh golfer, was put at the disposal of the Morrises. By crossing the Firth of Forth, they were saved the railway journey through Edinburgh. As they walked from the harbour, a second telegram brought the news that his wife had died in childbirth. Young Tom never recovered from the shock. Three months later, he had dinner with a few friends on Christmas Eve and retired to bed, but died in his sleep on Christmas Day, 1875 at the age of twenty-four.

Soon after his death a memorial to his memory was made possible by public subscription. The committee

accepted the design by John Rhind, the Edinburgh sculptor, worked out in Binny freestone. In bas-relief, a figure of Young Tom, about three-quarter life-size, is shown in golf jacket and wearing a Scottish Glengarry. He addresses the ball with an iron, sizing up a wrist shot to the hole. The inscription was written by the Very Reverend Principal Tulloch, Dean of the Thistle and Vice-Chancellor of the University of St Andrews: 'In memory of "Tommy", son of Thomas Morris, who died 25th December 1875, aged twenty-four years. Deeply regretted by numerous friends and all golfers. He thrice in succession won the Champion belt and held it without rivalry, and yet without envy, his many amiable qualities being no less acknowledged than his golfing achievements. This monument has been erected by contributions from sixty golfing societies.' The memorial was unveiled on 25 September 1878 by Miss Phelps, on behalf of Mrs Hunter, Young Tom's sister.

It is impossible to compare performances of one generation with those of another. It is enough to say that talent begets talent, but genius is unique.

The cover of W.W. Tulloch's famous book on the life of Tom Morris.

CHAPTER 6
WOMEN GOLFERS AT St ANDREWS

WOMEN GOLFERS
AT St ANDREWS

ST ANDREWS GOLFERS are said to be chauvinistic about women's championship golf on the Old Course. Maybe the women are over-sensitive, though there is an element of truth in the criticism. Prejudices die slowly in masculine strongholds, but the attitude is better than it used to be. Patronising acceptance is nearer the mark. Golfing emancipation is slow. After all, it is less than a hundred years since Lord Wellwood voiced this opinion, 'We venture to suggest seventy or eighty yards as the average limit of a drive advisedly; not because we doubt a lady's power to make a longer drive, but because that cannot well be done without raising the club above the shoulder. Now, we do not presume to dictate, but we must observe that the posture and gestures requisite for a full swing are not particularly graceful when the player is clad in female dress.'

St Andrews must be given the credit for having a Ladies Golf Club as far back as 1867, with activities mainly on the putting green, but with Spring and Autumn Meetings on a short course. It must have been popular because nineteen years later membership had topped the 500 mark. Throughout the country, ladies' golf was an activity of the upper crust, enjoyed at fashionable resorts on a country-house-party basis. There were exceptions. A reference to ladies' golf in a minute of the Royal Musselburgh Golf Club dated 14 December 1810 records, 'The Club to present by sub-scription a handsome new Creel and Shawl to the best Female Golfer, who plays on the annual occasion on the 1st of January next, old style (12th January new), to be intimated to the Fish Ladies by William Robertson, the Officer of the Club.

'Two of the best Barcelona Silk Handkerchiefs to be added to the above praemium of the Creel.

(Signed) Alex. G. Hunter, Captain.'

On this evidence, the early women golfers were fishing girls. It conjures up the picture of the winner strolling that evening down Musselburgh High Street wearing the shawl, though examination of the minute suggests that *Shawl* was a misreading of *Skull*, a mistake repeated by accepting Robert Clark's interpretation without checking. If this is so, then the *skull* refers to a form of fishing basket.

It is safer to hie back to 1893 when the Ladies' Golf Union was formed. The idea originated with the Ladies' Section of the Royal Wimbledon Club, the cradle of women's competitive golf. Circulars were sent out by the committee inviting representatives from clubs who approved the suggestion of such a Union to attend a meeting in London on 19 April 1893. The clubs who accepted were a mixed bag: St Andrews, Great Harrowden Hill, Barnes, Eastbourne, Blackheath, Southdown and Brighton, Holywood, Minchinhampton, Ashdown

Forest, Wimbledon and Lytham St Anne's. It was decided the Union should be formed. Laidlaw Purves, chairman of the meeting, outlined in detail the advantages that would follow. Issette Pearson, an outstanding player of her generation, became honorary secretary, and was largely responsible for the LGU system of universal handicapping.

Despite the handicap of unsuitable clothes and clumsy equipment, several players were prominent before the century drew to a close, the most outstanding being Lady Margaret Scott, daughter of the third Earl of Eldon, who dominated the first three championships and then appeared no more in major competitive golf. As regards St Andrews, the opening of the Jubilee Course in 1897 was welcomed by women who were tired of the restrictions of glorified putting greens. The breakthrough came in 1898 when St Rule's Ladies' Golf Club came into being. Five years later, the members organised the first Ladies' Golf Championship of Scotland which was held on the Old Course and won by Alice Glover by one hole against Margaret Graham. Since then this Championship has been half-a-dozen times to St Andrews, producing such doughty champions as Mrs J. B. Watson and Helen Holm. The British Ladies' Open Championship has been decided four times on the Old Course. In 1975 the title went to America after Mrs N. Syms beat Miss S. Cadden by 3 and 2. Ten years before it had been the turn of France, Brigit Varangot accounting for Belle Robertson in the final by 4 and 3. The two previous occasions on the Old Course had been in 1929 and 1908. The last was hailed as a break-through on a links traditionally associated with the stronger sex and when, for the first time in LGU history, the Union flag flew from the Royal and Ancient mast, even Mrs Pankhurst would have been pleased. Masculine reaction has mellowed since those early days, but there is still a die-hard trace of irritation, a refusal to accept that women's prowess on the Old Course is worthy of attention.

The attitude of royal golfers has been more courteous and understanding. As far back as 1876 when Prince Leopold, a younger son of Queen Victoria, was at St Andrews for the ceremony of driving himself in as Captain of the Royal and Ancient, he watched the ladies playing in a competition and afterwards sent a special prize to the winner. In 1922, the Prince of Wales, later Duke of Windsor, took part in the traditional installation as Captain of the Royal and Ancient, then had afternoon tea in the Ladies' Club and presented silver cups to Mrs Benson and Mrs MacAllen, the winner and runner-up of a women's competition held that day. The Duke of York, later King George VI, continued the tradition in 1930. Queen Elizabeth II is Patron of the Royal and Ancient Golf Club and her portrait by Pietro Annigoni hangs in a place of honour in the Big Room. The younger members of the Royal family have not become golf conscious, though Princess Anne opened the Old Course Golf and Country Club in 1983. Six years earlier the feminine touch was officially recognised in St Andrews when the Ladies' Golf Union headquarters moved into premises overlooking the last green.

So much attention has been devoted to historic triumphs on the Old Course involving names like Severiano Ballesteros, Jack Nicklaus, Tony Lema, Kel Nagle, Peter Thomson, Bobby Locke, Sam Snead, Richard Burton, Densmore Shute, Bobby Jones, James Braid, J. H. Taylor – and from the dim past men like Tom Kidd, Bob Martin and Jamie Anderson – that the achievements by women on the few occasions when they have played under championship conditions on the Old Course are overlooked and forgotten. Rarely is the Ladies' Open of 1908 recalled, yet it marked the emergence of one of Britain's finest women golfers. Seventeen-year-old Cecil Leitch began by beating a strong American by 9 and 8 and continued the winning sequence through several rounds, only to lose at the eighteenth in her semi-final match against the favourite, Maud Titterton, who went on to win the title. It was an excellent debut by a youngster who was to win the Championship on several occasions, but nothing before or since has equalled the brilliance of the golf seen in the 1929 Ladies' Open at St Andrews. It was one that male sceptics would do well to remember.

During the period when women's golf had to vie with the headline performances of such men as Walter Hagen, Gene Sarazen, Bobby Jones and Tommy Armour, the superb style and impressive record of Joyce Wethered, later Lady Heathcoat Amory, was not as widely acclaimed as it might have been. Now she is remembered as a legendary shadow in the record book whose victories were gained in a different era. But even allowing for changes in playing standards and equipment, I would still rank Joyce Wethered as the greatest golfer in the history of British women's golf. Her technique was dateless. Head and shoulders above her contemporaries who were beginning to break the eighty barrier, she regularly returned 72s and 73s. Her style was fluent; she took the club back inside the line of flight with a slightly more restricted hip pivot than the shoulder pivot and a shift of the hips to the left at the start of the downswing. Drives were played with a fairly full swing and a big arc, aided by her height. Incisive iron shots took a low trajectory with hands taken back only shoulder-high and finishing no higher than her shoulders. She outdistanced opponents without giving the impression of hitting hard. Her timing was remarkable. Total concentration gave her an air of aloofness. No doubt her early training helped. As an adolescent, she played at Dornoch where the family had a house near the links, while match-play experience came from playing against her equally famous brother, Roger.

Joyce Wethered showing one of the most famous of grips — firm but without poker-like tension. Placement repays study.

Joyce Wethered's swing. Note both heels are off the ground at impact. This mannerism is contrary to orthodox teaching but has become a feature of several top-ranking players. It is an unconscious counter to the pull of the swing.

Joyce Wethered's record spoke for itself. She entered for six British Ladies' Open Championships and won the title four times; played in five consecutive English Championships and won them all; claimed the Worplesdon Mixed Foursomes on eight occasions, seven with different partners and twice with Cyril Tolley. After her third victory in the Ladies' Open, Joyce quitted competitive golf, but changed her mind when St Andrews was named as the venue for the Championship. Her greatest ambition was to win the title on the Old Course, so once again she entered the fray. Her opponent in the final was the greatest American woman golfer of that era, Glenna Collett, later Glenna Vare. It was a clash between two outstanding champions, a repeat of their match in the third round of the 1925 British Ladies' Open at Troon. The American girl stood one over par after fifteen holes, but by then it was over by 4 and 3, Joyce Wethered having carded the last ten holes in six under par.

The return match four years later at St Andrews produced the finest final in the history of this Championship. Watched by a crowd estimated at 10,000, in perfect weather conditions, Glenna Collett went out in 34 and was three under fours for eleven holes, an inspired streak that included a two, a three and nine fours. At that point Joyce Wethered was five down, largely due to hesitant putting. Glenna missed from four feet at the twelfth. Joyce fought back and went into lunch two down. By the third hole in the afternoon the match was all-square. Out in 35 the English girl was four up, but her opponent retaliated and won the next two holes with threes. Two up with seven to go, it was anyone's match. Nerves affected both players at the Long Hole In, which was the only indifferent hole of the day. The fifteenth saw Joyce sink a five-yard uphill putt to become two up with three to play. The climax came at the 35th with Joyce Wethered winning by 3 and 1.

Scores on the final day

Glenna Collett (morning)	4-4-4-4-4-4-4-2-4 – 34
	4-3-5-4-6-4-5-5-5 – 41
	75
Joyce Wethered (morning)	5-5-3-4-5-4-5-3-5 – 39
	4-3-5-4-5-4-4-5-4 – 38
	77
Glenna Collett (afternoon)	4-5-5-5-4-6-5-4-4 – 42
	3-3-4-5-7-4-4-6 36 for 8
Joyce Wethered (afternoon)	3-5-4-4-5-4-4-3-3 – 35
	4-4-4-4-8-4-4-5 – 37 for 8

Glenna Collett, America's greatest amateur woman golfer, who set a new standard for her fellow countrywomen.

So ended the remarkable playing career of Joyce Wethered after a match on a par with any final seen on the Old Course. Women's championships have not been plentiful at St Andrews, but those held coincided with the Leitch and Wethered classic eras, reminders that the Ladies' Golf Union has made significant contributions to the history of the game on the Old Course. When the British Ladies' Open is held at St Andrews, it has become customary for the Royal and Ancient to hold an evening 'At Home' and allow the competitors to inspect the famous trophies, medals and regalia. Naturally such a gesture is appreciated, but even in this masculine stronghold more emphasis might be made of the position that women golfers occupy in the evolution of the game.

CHAPTER 7

CHAMPIONS ALL

CHAMPIONS ALL

ALL THESE players won fame at St Andrews. Each one went away with either the Open or Amateur Championship title in his luggage. The recollection of some of their achievements, like those of Severiano Ballesteros and Jack Nicklaus, is still fresh, but many others have slipped through the 'mellowing glass' of memory. We realise with astonishment that years have passed since we heard their names. At one time they seemed as much a part of the permanent scheme of things as the Old Course that forms the background to their victories, but then it was time for them to go. Their skills became obscured by new names, new methods, new standards. Fame is as fleeting as ever. It is therefore appropriate to recall something of their prowess over the years on the Old Course of St Andrews.

The famous Open Championship trophy.

Tom Kidd
1873

The first Open Championship to be played at St Andrews was in 1873. Prior to that, Prestwick had been the venue since the event was inaugurated in 1860 by the home club. A Champion Belt was the challenge prize to be contested annually, open to all golfers, amateur or professional, thirty-six holes to be played, or three rounds of the twelve-hole Prestwick course. The Belt would become the absolute property of any golfer who won it three times in succession. Young Tom Morris did so in the years 1868–70. The Championship was not held the following year. The Belt was replaced by the Cup, a joint gift of St Andrews, Prestwick and Musselburgh, and would be contested over 36 holes over these three links in annual rotation. Young Tom took over where he left off and had his name inscribed on the trophy after his fourth consecutive victory. That sequence was broken by Tom Kidd, a St Andrews caddie who was a manservant after play. His winning aggregate of 179 seems very high as contemporary reports record that the weather was perfect on the Old Course, yet nobody was able to take advantage.

Robert Martin
1876 and 1885

The 1876 Open Championship produced several surprises. The title could so easily have gone to J. O. F. Morris, the youngest son of Old Tom, who named him after Colonel John Ogilvie Fairlie of Goodham, which became shortened to *Jof*. Two sixes would have been sufficient, but nine at the seventeenth and six at the home hole ruined his chances. David Strath, younger brother of Andrew, also threw away his chances. At the Long Hole In his drive struck another St Andrews player. Concentration was affected and shots were dropped, then at the seventeenth Bob Martin's supporters claimed that Strath had played to the green before the match ahead had left the green. The Championship ended with a tie between Bob Martin and David Strath on 176. A protest was lodged by Martin. The Club declared there should be a play-off. Strath appealed and refused to compete until his case had been heard. No decision was given. Strath declined to play. Bob Martin was declared the Champion. Strath won £5 as runner-up. Time evened matters. Bob Martin is forgotten, just an entry in the record-book, but the name of Strath is still remembered in the Strath bunker by the eleventh green, though those caught in its depths are probably unaware of the famous St Andrews professional who died of consumption at the age of 39.

Bob Martin won the Open title for the second time in 1885, also at St Andrews. This time there were no controversial incidents, though the finish was close: 171 to 172 by Archie Simpson, one of the strongest of those early professionals who never won the Open. This time he had the advantage of length. At the sixth he was credited with a drive of 360 yards which was some feat with the old guttie ball, but Martin's plodding consistency won the day.

Jamie Anderson
1879

Jamie Anderson won three consecutive Open Championships from 1877, the last occasion being at St Andrews, where he was born in 1842. He was the son of Old Daw, one of the many colourful caddies who were part of the Scottish golfing scene last century. When his playing days were over, Old Daw used to push a home-made cart round the Old Course offering liquid refreshment to tiring golfers. Jamie's golfing career began at the age of ten. As a professional he was noted for his accuracy rather than length and became a putter of rare skill. He boasted of having played 100 consecutive shots on the Old Course without once deviating from the line. His winning aggregate in the 1879 Open was 170. After a period as professional to the Ardeer Golf Club in Ayrshire, he returned and settled in St Andrews.

Bob Ferguson
1882

This naturally-gifted golfer was born at Musselburgh in 1848 and learnt the game the hard way. He was a caddie from the age of eight. Ten years later, he competed against the leading professionals and won the Leith Tournament. During the next three years he beat Tom Morris six times, the equivalent of an up-and-coming youngster today beating Tom Watson. We read how he and young Tom Morris, representing England in a foursome match, beat the Scottish pairing of Bob Kirk and John Allan at Hoylake. Ferguson won the Open title in 1880, 1881 and 1882, the last occasion at St Andrews with a score of 171. He might have made it four in a row the following year when he tied with Willie Fernie, but lost the play-off. That was Ferguson's last success in the Championship. Shortly afterwards he contracted typhoid and never fully recovered. In the same way that St Andrews remembered George John Whyte-Melville with a fountain set in cobblestones in Market Street, where the Mercat Cross once stood, so Bob Ferguson is recalled by a fountain erected by the Musselburgh Links.

'The grounds on which golf is played are called links being the barren, sandy soil from which the sea has retired in recent geological times. In their natural state links are covered with long, rank, benty grass and gorse. . . . Links are too barren for cultivation; but sheep, rabbits, geese and professionals pick up a precarious livelihood on them.'

Sir W. G. Simpson. *The Art of Golf*, 1892

Horace Hutchinson
1886

Horace Hutchinson exercised considerable influence on the development of golf in England at the close of last century. Flamboyant, picturesque, at times temperamental, he had the personality and skill to command attention. He was a genuine pioneer. Born in London on 16 May 1859, Hutchinson took to golf at Westward Ho at the age of thirteen. He learnt quickly. Purists criticised his style of the raised right elbow and dipped right knee as potential faults, but results silenced critics. He reached the final of the Amateur Championship three years in succession, was runner-up in the inaugural Championship at Hoylake in 1885, semi-finalist 1896, 1901 and 1904 and finalist in 1903, only to be beaten by Robert Maxwell by 7 and 5. Ill-health curtailed his final years. He died in London in 1932.

Of his many triumphs, it is appropriate to recall the victory in the first Amateur Championship to be held at St Andrews in September 1886. Everything was fresh. It had been arranged that the Championship should be held annually over the links of St Andrews, Hoylake and Prestwick, clubs that provided funds to purchase a champion trophy at a cost of £100 with a gold medal for the winner, who would be 'permitted to appropriate the title of Amateur Champion without anyone daring to say him nay.' In such a simple way did this Championship come into being, like spring breaking into bud, gradually blooming into the fullness of its maturity today. Those September days of 1886 seem far away. Had George Borrow been a golfer, he might have reflected, 'How for everything there is a time and a season and then how does the glory of a thing pass from it even like the flower of the grass'. Horace Hutchinson experienced that freshness. He spanned the years. When he was born, none of the Championships had been conceived. The year he died our Open Champion was Gene Sarazen, the Amateur Champion was John de Forest. But in spirit Hutchinson belonged to the early days. Looking down the list of entries for that 1886 St Andrews Championship, one sees many familiar names. Their efforts during those three autumn days by the Eden are forgotten, but can once more be remembered.

First Round

Marcus J. Brown beat C. M. Smith 4 and 2
H. S. C. Everard beat J. L. Luke 7 and 6
D. Argyll-Robertson beat H. B. Simpson 3 and 2
R. Gilroy beat John Dun (absent)
John Ball *tertius* beat H. F. Caldwell 3 and 2
Gregor MacGregor beat T. Gilroy 1 up
S. C. Fowler beat Jas. Cullen (absent)
J. E. Laidlay beat W. R. Kermack 3 and 2
Col. Boothby beat W. Gibson-Bloxsom 7 and 6
A. F. Macfie beat Jas. Duncan 4 and 3

Second Round

J. Cunningham, jun., beat David Brown (absent)
W. H. De Zoete beat A. M. Ross 3 and 1
E. S. Balfour beat P. D. Mitchell 6 and 4
C. Chambers beat David L. Lamb 3 and 2
S. Mure-Fergusson beat C. S. Carnegie 5 and 4
J. Penn beat Kenneth Macdonald 3 and 1
D. McCuaig beat J. Foggo 1 up
Horace G. Hutchinson beat G. M. Cox (absent)
F. H. Maitland Dougall beat Capt. W. H. Burn 1 up
Leslie M. Balfour beat J. G. Tait 2 and 1
H. A. Lamb beat Charles Anderson 2 and 1
H. S. C. Everard beat Marcus J. Brown 9 and 8
R. Gilroy beat D. Argyll Robertson 3 and 2

John Ball *tertius* beat Gregor MacGregor 7 and 6
J. E. Laidlay beat S. C. Fowler 6 and 5
A. F. Macfie beat Col. Boothby 6 and 4

Third Round

J. Cunningham, jun., beat W. H. De Zoete 3 and 2
C. Chambers beat E. S. Balfour 5 and 4
S. Mure Fergusson beat J. Penn 2 up
Horace G. Hutchinson beat Dr. D. McCuaig 8 and 7
Leslie M. Balfour beat F. H. Maitland Dougall 4 and 3
H. A. Lamb beat H. S. C. Everard 3 and 1
John Ball *tertius* beat T. Gilroy 6 and 4
J. E. Laidlay beat A. F. Macfie 1 up.

Fourth Round

C. Chambers beat J. Cunningham, jun., 4 and 2
Horace G. Hutchinson beat S. Mure Fergusson 1 up
H. A. Lamb beat Leslie M. Balfour 1 up
John Ball *tertius* beat J. E. Laidlay 3 and 2

Fifth Round

Horace G., Hutchinson beat C. Chambers 5 and 3
H. A. Lamb beat John Ball *tertius* 7 and 6

Final Round

Horace G. Hutchinson beat H. A. Lamb 7 and 6

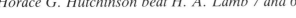

The British Amateur Championship trophy.

Hutchinson was a man of many interests. A prolific writer, his range of subjects was wide. Golfing matters were dealt with in authoritative fashion, not only about contemporary personalities but on the techniques of the swing. Otherwise, his tastes were catholic. A complete set of his books would be a collector's item. It would include such titles as *Hints on Golf*, *Cricketing Saws and Stories*, *Golf* in the *Badminton Library*, *Shooting*, *Little Lady Mary*, *The Book of Golf and Golfers*, *My Wife's Politics*, *Fifty Years of Golf*, *Nature's Moods and Tenses*, *The Fortnightly Club*, *Bert Edward, the Golf Caddie*, *The New Forest*, *Peter Steele the Cricketer*, *Two Moods of a Man*, *Mr Punt of Chelsea*, *Portraits of the Eighties*, and many others. With such odd companions in juxtaposition, it is appropriate to end with one of his innumerable observations:

'It is a thousand pities that neither Aristotle nor Shakespeare was a golfer. There is no other game that strips the soul so naked.'

Horace Hutchinson, flamboyant and temperamental winner of the first British Amateur Championship staged at St Andrews.

Jack Burns
1888

Little is known about Jack Burns except that he won the Open Championship at St Andrews in 1888. Contemporary sources record that he was born there in 1859, received his first lesson on golf from Young Tom Morris at the age of ten, worked as a plasterer in the town, later became greenkeeper and professional at Warwick Golf Club and played in the first Open staged at St Andrews in 1885, finishing fourth, four shots behind Bob Martin. The 1888 Open attracted an entry of 52 and included amateurs like Leslie Balfour, J. E. Laidlay, H. S. C. Everard and A. F. Macfie. Gale-force winds and almost arctic conditions caused scores to soar. In the first round Willie Park, the defending champion, returned 90, nor could men like Laidlay (93), Fernie (91), Everard (93) and Tom Morris (94) cope with the conditions. Willie Campbell was leader with 84 followed by Ben Sayers (85) and Jack Burns (87).

The afternoon was even worse. Campbell slumped with 90 alongside Laidlay, Willie Park was 92, and Jamie Anderson narrowly missed a century with 99. At the end of the day David Anderson, Jr., Ben Sayers and Jack Burns tied on 172, until it was discovered that Burns's morning round had been 86 not 87 which made the native of St Andrews Open champion. He received a commemorative medal and £8 prize money. Sayers and Anderson pooled the second and third purses of £6 and £3. Campbell was enriched by £2. D. Grant and Andrew Kirkaldy tied for fifth place, played-off the next day. Sayers returned 100 whilst Campbell's 87 earned £1.

An observer noted: 'the competition, on the whole, was a most successful one, but that such a mistake as that which took place with the winning score was possible, clearly demonstrates that in future arrangements should be made by which the cards should be collected and checked by some responsible person.' Jack Burns was given a character reference: '. . . steady in his conduct, respectful in his demeanour and honest in all his transactions, a worthy recipient of the highest honours which the golfing world can bestow.' Such ambitions were never realised. Later, he returned to St Andrews and worked as a platelayer on the railway line.

J. Burns	86–85 – 171
D. Anderson, Jr.	86–86 – 172
B. Sayers	85–87 – 172
W. Campbell	84–90 – 174
Mr. Leslie Balfour	86–89 – 175
A. Kirkaldy	87–89 – 176
A. Herd	93–84 – 177
Mr. A. F. Macfie	94–91 – 185
Tom Morris	94–96 – 190
J. Anderson	96–99 – 195

J. E. Laidlay
1889 and 1891

The 1889 Amateur Championship attracted an entry of 40 and was played over the Old Course in perfect conditions without wind or rain. J. E. Laidlay's progress to the final was at the expense of F. C. Crawford (8 and 7); Harold Hilton, making his first visit to St Andrews, by one hole; Alan Macfie by 2 and 1, and John Ball at the twentieth. In the final, Laidlay played Leslie Balfour, took the lead at the third, never lost it and won by 2 and 1. At that time Laidlay was a dominant force in amateur golf. He won the Amateur Championship twice, was three times runner-up, and narrowly missed winning the Open in 1893. Born at Seacliff, Haddingtonshire in 1860, Laidlay went to Loretto School at the age of twelve and took to golf two years later. The records are sprinkled with Laidlay rounds which in those days were remarkably low. At Musselburgh in 1876 in a three-ball match, he carded the two rounds in 72. St Andrews, Hoylake and Carnoustie were played in 77. At North Berwick he returned 70 with an outward half that included one two and six threes. Luffness was completed in 69. Today such scores are commonplace, but then the equipment and balls used, together with the state of the links, made such low scoring outstanding. His style was unorthodox in that he drew his weight away from the ball in the backswing, bringing it back at impact. It suited him, but was not one to copy. Apart from golf, Laidlay made his mark at cricket. At sixteen, he played for the Gentlemen of Scotland against the Yorkshire County side and claimed eleven wickets for 73 with his slow bowling.

J. E. Laidlay (right), a dominant force in amateur golf, who beat John Ball at the 20th in the 1889 Amateur Championship

Hugh Kirkaldy
1891

Hugh Kirkaldy had the distinction of winning the last Open Championship to be decided over 36 holes. That was at St Andrews in 1891 when two rounds of 83 lowered the Championship aggregate record by four strokes, in spite of stormy conditions. Kirkaldy's knowledge of the Old Course and its climatic vagaries minimised many of its terrors. He was the first to beat Young Tom Morris's record of 77. On another occasion his slashing style gave him a remarkable outward half of 4–4–4–4–4–4–3–2–4 – 33. An inward half of 41 enabled him to beat Ben Sayers by 7 and 6. Nine months later, Kirkaldy went around the Old Course in 35 out, 38 in; the 73 remained the course record until beaten by F. G. Tait in 1894.

In the 1892 Open, he was bracketed with John Ball and Sandy Herd in second place. The next year he finished fourth, four strokes behind the winner, Willie Auchterlonie. He won an important tournament at Musselburgh shortly afterwards, two shots ahead of his brother Andrew. Kirkaldy's last appearance in the Open was in 1895 at St Andrews, where he finished fifteenth with rounds of 87–87–83–84. In 1896 he played J. H. Taylor, then champion, for two days at Silloth. The first day left them level at 151 after 36 holes. On the second, Kirkaldy won decisively by 4 and 3. Some time later, he caught influenza, developed consumption and died aged 29.

Hugh Kirkaldy was type-cast of the early rugged school of brusque Scottish professionals who learnt their craft as caddies, traits shared by his brothers, particularly Andrew.

Leslie Balfour-Melville
1895

Amateur golfers in the early days played with gusto. Shot-making was individualistic, clubs and balls unpredictable, links and greens often rough. Even so, men like Harold Hilton, John Ball, Horace Hutchinson, J. E. Laidlay and Mure Fergusson produced shots that were nothing short of brilliant. Given modern sophisticated equipment, results might have been remarkable. One such amateur was Leslie Balfour-Melville, an all-round sportsman who was a natural athlete and played cricket for the Gentlemen of Scotland, but golf was his first choice. He was essentially a St Andrews man. The list of his wins reads like a catalogue of Royal and Ancient medals, along with victories at the Honourable Company of Edinburgh Golfers and Musselburgh, but the Old Course was where he excelled. It was at St Andrews in 1895 that he not only won the Amateur Championship but in the final beat John Ball at the nineteenth, after a closely contested match in which the Swilcan Burn played a prominent role.

J. H. Taylor
1895 and 1900

As far as I know, there is no statue in England to J. H. Taylor. Had he been born across the Atlantic, we should probably see him gazing with leaden eyes across some famous golf course or holding a bronze iron in one of the rooms of the American PGA headquarters. Instead we took his five Open Championship wins in our stride, and rely on pen portraits of the sturdy figure with massive boots anchored to the ground, cap jammed down and protruding chin. The swing, somewhat curtailed, was flat-footed, the right foot slightly forward, with drives that ruled the pin. Temperamentally there was nothing of the stoical, poker-faced pose. Few men had to quell such inner flames. He was acknowledged as the senior statesman of golf, a professional who did more than any man to improve the status of his colleagues.

In 1951 the BBC arranged for a programme of his reminiscences. Since he was unwilling to leave the quiet of Westward Ho, the unit travelled to Devon. Technicians converted his sitting-room into a studio. The microphone was installed on a desk which he told me had been presented to him by the Artisan Golfers' Association. He recalled many triumphs, and high on the list were the Open Championship victories at St Andrews in 1895 and 1900. He had the satisfaction of being the first English-born professional to win the Open title, a fact that had wounded Scottish pride. He spoke of his childhood at Northam, the village by the Westward Ho links where he was born in 1871. As a lad he caddied, then worked for the club professionals, Johnnie, Mat and Jamie Allan. He carried clubs regularly for Horace Hutchinson, from whom he picked up many a useful tip, and talked of the day when he beat the famous amateur by one hole.

He lived again the matches against Harry Vardon, James Braid and Sandy Herd, but his victory at St Andrews in 1895 was a highlight. Vardon had the lowest score for the first round, but in the end could only tie for ninth place while J.H. recorded his second Open win in succession. The next year Vardon had his revenge at Muirfield. Prior to the championship, Vardon played a challenge match against Taylor over 36 holes and won by 8 and 6. In the Open both men tied on 316, Vardon narrowly winning the play-off for his first Championship victory. Over the next three years, Vardon won twice more, but J.H. countered at St Andrews in 1900, becoming Champion with an aggregate of 309.

Taylor's affection for the Old Course was deep. He said that given the choice of a links on which to play an important match, he would have chosen St Andrews. He felt it was a stern but fair examination and demanded the right temperament. It had to be tackled intelligently, but could be a chastening experience. It was a true test of skill and character.

J.H. Taylor always regarded the Old Course as a stern but fair examination.

John Ball and Harold Hilton
1901, 1907 and 1913

Of those who have won the Amateur Championship at St Andrews, one of the greatest was John Ball. Between 1888 and 1912 he held the title eight times. He was the first amateur to win the Open. He captained England against Scotland from 1902 to 1911. When the South African war broke out, he was Amateur Champion. He served in that campaign and again in World War I. He played in his last Amateur Championship in 1921 in his sixty-first year. In the 1907 Amateur at St Andrews, he beat C. A. Palmer in the final by 6 and 4.

In spite of these victories, John Ball remained retiring and aloof. He seldom talked of his success. After his St Andrews win, the population of the fishing village of Hoylake planned to give him a welcome at the station and escort him to the Royal Hotel. Ball heard of these preparations and left the train at Meols, the station before Hoylake, and walked home alone along the deserted foreshore. This modesty was not assumed but was part of his nature. When he was playing, the gallery did not bother him, but after it was over he withdrew into his shell. I turned up a letter I received from J. H. Taylor over forty years ago in which he compared Harry Vardon and John Ball. 'Both had the killer instinct but with this difference. Vardon smiled during the process whilst Johnnie set about the job gloomily silent and apparently contemptuous as if pitying the unfortunate who was opposing him. Let me hasten to soften the unmeant harshness of this stricture on an old friend who congratulated me as I stepped forward to receive my first Championship Medal at Sandwich in 1894 by saying that Johnnie if reserved would show appreciation of an opponent's skill by a nod of the head which was more eloquent than mere words. Both Vardon and Ball were equally resolved in intention to win by similar methods of attack. Their records prove that the end justified the means they employed with such deadly effect.'

John Ball's main rival was Harold Hilton, the second member of the famous Hoylake Triumvirate, whose record of winning both the Open and Amateur Championships on two occasions and the American Amateur Championship once would have made him the outstanding player of his period had he not had the misfortune to run parallel with the era of Ball's greatness. He was one of our finest score players. The present generation knows Hilton by legend and fact, by photographs, by record books, by the amusing way in which his cap used to fall off as his club came through. But not many can trace his playing career in detail. Very briefly, I shall sketch his golfing record up to the beginning of this century.

Hilton learned his golf at Hoylake. His early life was closely associated with the game. Apart from living close to the links, his day school turned out such golfers as John Ball, the Crowthers, Herbert Tweedie and W. More. Hilton was eight years of age when he made his first competitive appearance. It was the competition at Hoylake for boys under sixteen, who played the full eighteen holes, and the boys under twelve who played only twelve holes. Over-ambitious, Hilton entered for the major event and was out of his depth. The next year he entered the junior section and won the first prize from scratch, following it the next season by winning the senior scratch medal. In the spring of 1887, Hilton joined the Royal Liverpool Golf Club, the season that the Amateur Championship was held at Hoylake. The small entry of 33 included for the first time the name of Harold Hilton. He reached the second round, only to be beaten by John Ball, Senior. His next appearance was

even shorter-lived. J. E. Laidlay defeated him on the last green in the first round. In 1889 the Amateur went to St Andrews. The title went to Laidlay who beat L. M. B. Melville in the final by 2 and 1.

It was held at Hoylake again in 1890. This time Hilton survived three rounds before losing to John Ball on the sixteenth green. St Andrews 1891 was his chance to win his first Amateur Championship, but it was snatched away by his rival, J. E. Laidlay, who won at the twentieth in the final. Hilton made his bow in the Open Championship the same year also over the Old Course and finished second amateur to Mure Fergusson. Hilton's first outstanding season was in 1892. In the Amateur he beat Laidlay in the first round, but lost in the final to John Ball at the seventeenth. He was undecided about playing in the Open. His parents and his employer were opposed, but he decided in favour and went on the night train to Scotland. There was time for only one day's practice so he crammed in three rounds. An opening round of 78 left him four shots behind the leader, Horace Hutchinson. A second round of 81 left him trailing by eight strokes, but 72 in the third round lifted him to second place, three behind Ball. In the final round he needed eight at the last hole to take the title. He took six.

Hilton added many more honours, but always had to overcome fierce opposition from Ball, Laidlay, and particularly Freddie Tait who beat him on many occasions. He used to say that the Scot was the only player he feared. In the Amateur Championship at St Andrews in 1895, Hilton was handicapped by a wrist injury, but beat C. E. Dick in the first round, then lost at the sixteenth in the second round against Willie Greig. He also slumped badly in the Open on the Old Course where bad luck robbed Sandy Herd of victory, the title going to J. H.

Taylor for the second year in succession. Hilton won the Amateur Championship in 1900 after twelve years of endeavour. There were two regrettable gaps in the entry. Freddie Tait had died and John Ball was still in South Africa, but Hilton's victims included Robert Maxwell and John Robb, whom he beat in the final by 8 and 7. The following year the Old Course saw Hilton retain the Amateur title by defeating John Low by one hole. He was to become Amateur Champion twice more, in 1911 and 1913 and won the American amateur title in 1911.

Both John Ball and Harold Hilton were rare golfers. I recall the last appearance of both men in the Amateur Championship. Each had 99 matches to his credit in this event. Everybody hoped that the sweetness of one more victory might fall to their lot in their final championship. It was not to be. Both were defeated, and having reached the century mark their championship careers closed. Both are dead, but to many of an older generation the mention of John Ball recalls memories of a silent golfer with a slight stoop striding across the links in the dusk of a summer evening followed by the wizened little caddie who always accompanied him.

John Ball won the Amateur Championship title eight times between 1885 and 1912 and was the first amateur to win the Open Championship.

James Braid
1905 and 1910

James Braid won the Open Championship for the first time in 1901. In the short space of a decade he claimed the title five times, twice on the Old Course. In 1905 the entry was 152. Bad weather affected play, but Braid's rounds of 81–78–78–81 were good enough to take the Championship in spite of sixes at the fifteenth and sixteenth. On both occasions he drove out-of-bounds and had to play from difficult lies on the railway track. In 1910, a thunderstorm disrupted play with flooded bunkers and submerged greens, but Braid completed the round in spite of lashing rain and lightning, handing in a card of 77 which he always regarded as the finest round of his career. Unfortunately, the Old Course was pronounced unplayable and the round was discarded.

Nevertheless he went on to win with an aggregate of 299.

Braid died in London on 27 November 1950 at the age of eighty. One of the few remaining giants of the last century, he formed the Triumvirate with J. H. Taylor and Harry Vardon and monopolised British professional golf for twenty years. He was the first to win the Open five times, which was later equalled by Taylor and beaten by Vardon. A tall, exceptionally powerful player, he was noted for long driving and remarkable powers of recovery that became legendary in his lifetime. His style was individual. He held a record of returning a birthday round in a score lower than his age until the eightieth birthday saw him fail by a single stroke. He was one of the founder members of the Professional Golfers' Association and was the first professional to be elected honorary member of his club. To that distinction was added the honour of being made a member of the Royal and Ancient Club, along with J. H. Taylor and Willie Auchterlonie. Hazlitt's well-known words about Cavanagh, the fives player, are appropriate: 'He had no affection, no trifling. He did not throw away the game to show off an attitude, or try and experiment. He was a fine, sensible, manly player, who did what he could.'

Left:
An interesting foursome with Harry Vardon, James Braid, Willie Fernie and J.H. Taylor.

James Braid with an oddly-shaped putter that belonged to the Australian professional, Bill Shankland.

Jock Hutchison
1921

The Open Championship of 1921 was packed with incident and developed into one of the most exciting seen on the Old Course. It was the first time that the Cup crossed the Atlantic. The winner, Jock Hutchison, was a St Andrews golfer, born and bred, but had emigrated, taken American citizenship and returned with his game thoroughly Americanised in style. He began as favourite and lived up to the compliment. He led the first round with a 72 which almost included two successive holes in one. At the eighth the teeshot was holed, then he came within inches of repeating the feat at the ninth – some 300 yards long. Had a spectator not rushed on to the green to remove the flag, the ball might have gone in. At the end of the day, Hutchison led by two strokes from George Duncan, the holder, Arnaud Massey, Tom Kerrigan, Jim Barnes and Walter Hagen.

The second round saw Hutchison maintain the lead with a 75. Barnes moved into second place one shot behind with 74, followed by Duncan and Sandy Herd. Wethered returned 75, but still trailed by six strokes. There was a change of lead in the third round. The veteran Sandy Herd, to the delight of St Andrews supporters, went to the front with 222 alongside Barnes, who had a 74. Wethered improved with 72 and was bracketed with Hagen on 223. Hutchison faltered; 79 left him on the 226-mark with Kerrigan. On the last day understanding officialdom granted Wethered's request to switch from a late starting-time to an earlier slot as he had arranged to play in a cricket match in the south the next day. There was a touch of resentment among the professionals, who argued that everybody should accept the luck of the draw. Another talking-point was the penalty Wethered had incurred in the third round. At the fourteenth hole he had gone forward to size up the next shot, stepped back and trodden on his own ball, incurring the penalty which some argued cost the amateur the title. That argument was shaky. It could have been applied to Wethered's last round of 72 when he wasted the chance of a 70 by pitching short at the eighteenth and needed three more shots from the Valley of Sin. Barnes and Herd felt the pressure and dropped out of contention with eighties. Havers and Duncan might have taken the title but also faltered. Kerrigan came near with a 72. Hutchison was left needing a four at the last hole to tie. He made no mistake. In the play-off between the amateur and the professional, experience told. Wethered finished three shots behind in the morning round with 77 against 74 and still had a chance, but after lunch he could make no impression – 82 against 76 gave Hutchison a winning margin of nine strokes. The American domination of the Open had begun, maybe a trifle luckily but on the day conclusive.

One controversial incident occurred during the Championship. Hutchison had used a score-faced mashie which invoked criticism. It was felt he could adopt bold tactics confident that the ball would come back from the pitch. It was true, but the ploy was legitimate. As far back as the 1873 Open Championship at St Andrews, Tom Kidd obtained a similar result by hacking the ball with a knife to make it rough.

Jock Hutchison (USA)	72–75–79–70 – 296
Mr R. H. Wethered (R & A)	78–75–72–71 – 296
Replay: Hutchison	74–76 – 150
Wethered	77–82 – 159
Tom Kerrigan (USA)	74–80–72–72 – 298
Arthur Havers (West Lancs)	76–74–77–72 – 299
George Duncan (Hanger Hill)	74–75–78–74 – 301

Sir Ernest Holderness
1924

St Andrews 1924 produced an Amateur Championship which lacked international flavour. A final between two Englishmen can be a hard sell to a Scottish gallery, but neutrality is quickly forgotten when the quality of golf is high. Ernest Holderness was pre-World War I vintage; he played for Oxford in 1910, 1911 and 1912, and more than held his own against the top amateurs of that time. A fine striker of the ball, Holderness compensated for lack of length by split-pin accuracy and a delicate touch on the greens. Two years before he had won the Amateur title at Prestwick when he beat a Scot, John Caven, by one up. At one stage there was the possibility of a repeat match at St Andrews, but Caven was beaten by Eustace Storey for a place in the semi-final, much to the disappointment of the locals because he was a great favourite. He died at St Andrews in 1982.

The highlights of that 1924 week were mixed. The American challenge came from one man, Francis I. Brown, who lived in Hawaii. In the qualifying rounds he broke the New Course record with a 67 and then carded the Old Course in 70. In the Championship proper, he beat a formidable Hoylake golfer, Alan Graham, by 2 and 1, but was eliminated by the same margin by J. Bernie of Inverness. Harold Gillies attracted attention by the incredibly high tees from which he swept the ball away with deep-faced clubs. Those who tried the tees on the practice ground found that shot-making had become a lottery. Several players had purple patches. Denys Kyle had such a day when he beat Harry Braid at the twenty-first in the morning and then accounted for Cyril Tolley after lunch to reach the last eight. Roger Wethered, who started as favourite on the strength of his 1923 success at Deal, was anything but consistent. In the first round he beat E. A. Lassen by 8 and 7. In another

he went out in 33 including five successive threes around the loop, then took 43 for the same holes in the third round but still won. Harold Hilton, champion of 1900, 1901, 1911 and 1913, recorded 99 victories, but was denied the 100 when Noel Layton beat him by 6 and 5.

Eustace Storey, playing in his first Amateur Championship, was the Cambridge University captain and in his fourth year as a student. He was known by the odd stance he adopted on the green. He struck the ball from a point opposite his right toe with the left foot twisted behind the right. Would-be imitators almost ruptured themselves, but it worked for Storey. From six feet he was deadly, but it did not subdue Holderness in the final, which was played in heavy rain and wind. The scorecards tell their own story:

Holderness	4–5–5–5–5–4–4–3–4 – 39
Storey	3–5–4–4–5–5–4–3–3 – 36
	Storey 3 up
Holderness	4–5–4–4–6–4–5–5–4 – 41 – 80
Storey	4–4–6–5–6–4–5–5–5 – 44 – 80
	Storey 1 up
Holderness	4–5–4–5–5–4–3–3–5 – 38
Storey	4–7–4–6–5–4–5–3–4 – 42
	Holderness 1 up
Holderness	4–5–4–5–5–4–4
Storey	4–4–5–5–6–4–5
	Holderness won 3 and 2

Twice winner of the Championship in three years, Ernest Holderness was technically a week-end golfer who worked five days a week as a Civil Servant. He was the genuine Amateur Champion.

Bobby Jones
1927 and 1930

Many years after his retirement from competitive golf, Bobby Jones said that if he had been obliged to live in one place and play golf there only for the rest of his life, he would have chosen the Old Course. He went on record 'In my humble opinion, St Andrews is the most fascinating golf course I have ever played. There is always a way at St Andrews, although it is not always the obvious way, and in trying to find it, there is more to be learned on this British course than in playing a hundred ordinary American golf courses.'

There was no doubting his affection and respect for the Old Course, but it was somewhat muted at the outset. In the 1921 Open Championship, Jones had a disastrous third round. Out in 46, he took six at the tenth, bunkered at the eleventh where another six was added, tore up his card in exasperation and returned to the clubhouse. It was a different story six years later. He came to St Andrews defending the Open title he had won at St Annes in 1926, when seven of the first ten finishers were American. Jones showed devastating form – 68 in the first round, 32 out and 36 home, equalled the course record and took a four-shot lead over the field. The weather held throughout the week. Without wind, the Old Course was in docile mood. It suited Jones – 72 in the second round, followed by 73 and 72 gave him an aggregate of 285 and a six-shot victory. He led from start to finish and never looked in danger.

In 1930 the unbelievable became fact and golfing history was made, but to get it in perspective it is timely to outline something of Jones's record. The basis of his immaculate swing, which was classical in its rhythm, came from Stewart Maiden, a Carnoustie-born professional who laid the foundation of Jones's game and was at hand throughout his career. The style was unmistak-able, an effortless flowing Scottish swing, almost lazy in its execution. It looked natural but was the result of almost microscopic analysis, in contrast with Maiden's methods which were simplicity itself as Jones confirmed: 'It seemed that he merely stepped up to the ball and hit it, which to the end of my playing career was always a characteristic of my play.'

Superlatives are dangerous. They lead to extravagant claims, but in the case of Bobby Jones they can be used. He was the greatest golfer of all time. Statistics speak for themselves. American Open Champion 1923, 1926, 1929 and 1930; tied in 1925 and 1928, but lost the play-offs; second in 1922 and 1924. American Amateur Champion in 1924, 1925, 1927, 1928 and 1930; runner-up in 1919 and 1926. Open Champion in 1926, 1927 and 1930. Amateur Champion in 1930. Played for America in the Walker Cup Match from its inauguration in 1922 until 1930, as well as the 1921 unofficial match. Everything crystallised in that amazing 1930 season. Ambition became reality when Bobby Jones won the Open Championship at Hoylake, the American Open Championship at Interlachen, the Amateur Championship at St Andrews and the American Amateur Championship at Merion, plus a thirteen-shot win in a professional tournament at Augusta and his thirty-six-hole Walker Cup match at Sandwich. From April to September he played competitive golf in Britain and America and never finished below first place.

Opposite:
Bobby Jones receiving the Freedom of the City of St Andrews in 1958 from Provost Leonard. Only once before had an American been so honoured — he was Benjamin Franklin.

In this tally of victories, the one at St Andrews was crucial. Nothing came easy in that Amateur Championship. Several of the matches were cliff-hangers. In the first round his opponent was Syd Roper, an English artisan, who refused to be intimidated by the American's start of 3–4–3–2, the fourth in particular producing a remarkable bunker shot that holed out from 150 yards. Roper lost at the sixteenth when he was one over fours. The semi-final against another American, George Voigt, produced a needle match in which Jones was two down with five to play. Voigt faltered and drove out of bounds at the fourteenth, found a bunker at the sixteenth, but rallied at the Road Hole where Jones sank a difficult putt to halve the hole. Voigt acknowledged defeat at the home hole. But the decisive hole in the quadrilateral triumph was unquestionably the Road Hole in the fourth round clash with Cyril Tolley. Here was a match that had all the ingredients. On the one hand, the reigning British Amateur champion against the Open champion of America. Tolley, majestic, domineering, at times wayward in his shots but capable of colossal drives, and Jones, inevitably the favourite, calm and unruffled. It began with the Englishman making a mess of the opening hole, but squared at the second, became one up at the fourth, then one down by the eighth. The ninth saw Tolley crash an enormous drive some 300 yards to the green to square the match. Tolley threw away the short eleventh with a poor teeshot and fluffed pitch then put his third shot into the bunker. He made amends at the twelfth with a vast drive and won the hole. Bobby Jones had a birdie at the thirteenth. Tolley retaliated at the fourteenth with an eagle three, then three-putted the fifteenth, but squared again at the sixteenth where Jones's hopes foundered in a bunker.

The Road Hole was the turning-point and became the most controversial point of the championship. It could not happen today, when spectators are controlled. Then the galleries were more flexible, and not penned behind the dreaded wall. Tolley's second shot ended by the bunker guarding the green. Jones took an iron stronger than might have been expected, played a low flying shot that landed on the green, bounced once, struck a spectator on the chest and rebounded about ten feet from the hole. Bernard Darwin said: 'hundreds are prepared to take the oath that it would otherwise have been on the road, and an equal number of witnesses are quite certain that it would not.' Some critics maintained that it was deliberate strategy which paid dividends. This was strenuously denied afterwards by Jones, but Cyril told me some years later that maybe there was a grain of truth in the assertion. Tolley replied with a glorious pitch, Jones missed the putt, and the match was all square on the eighteenth tee. Both had useful drives. The hole was halved. Tolley's second at the nineteenth was hooked into the crowd past the Swilcan; Jones played a safe, orthodox second. Tolley rallied with a superb chip that finished about three feet from the hole. Jones read the putt well, finished inches from the pin and left a dead stymie. Tolley had no option but to loft the ball into the hole. He struck it well; it hit the side and stayed on the rim. Victory went to Jones, but it was a narrow escape. In fact the American always maintained that Tolley had played the better golf on that day, certainly unlike the match between these two great amateurs in the Walker Cup at St Andrews when Jones won by 12 and 11. The 1930 Championship final was something of an anticlimax. Roger Wethered never raised his game: four down at lunchtime, he lost by 7 and 6. Bobby Jones had won the title and went on to make history. After beating all opposition, professional and amateur, in Britain and America, he retired at the age of twenty-eight. It was a decision that saddened the golfing world, but the timing was impeccable. Not many champions withdraw at the peak.

Bobby Jones was a man of many parts. As a scholar, he had first-class honours in Law, English Literature and Mechanical Engineering. He had a legal practice in Atlanta, Georgia. With Clifford Roberts, he planned and developed the Augusta national course and inaugurated the Masters' Tournament. In 1956 Bobby Jones was made an Honorary Member of the Royal and Ancient Golf Club. Two years later he was non-playing captain of the American team in the inaugural match for the Eisenhower Trophy and during that visit he was given the Freedom of the Burgh of St Andrews. He received it from a wheel-chair to which he had been confined for many years because of a spinal complaint. He died on 18 December 1971. At the memorial service in St Andrews, the congregation included all representative golfing officials. One final tribute was the decision to name the tenth hole on the Old Course after this famous amateur golfer who was so beloved and respected in St Andrews.

1927 Open Championship

Bobby Jones (USA)	68–72–73–72 – 285	
Aubrey Boomer (France)	76–70–73–72 – 291	
Fred Robson	76–72–69–74 – 291	
Joe Kirkwood (USA)	72–72–75–74 – 293	
Ernest Whitcombe	74–73–73–73 – 293	
Charles Whitcombe	74–76–71–75 – 296	
Bert Hodson	72–70–81–74 – 297	
Arthur Havers	80–72–77–76 – 305	

Densmore Shute
1933

Before the 1933 Open began, the American threat was feared. The entry included the full strength of the US Ryder Cup team plus a formidable amateur in George Dunlap. The past record was dismal. In thirteen years the trophy had crossed the Atlantic twelve times. This time was no exception. Not only were five of the first six finishers American, but the tie and play-off was between two US Ryder Cup players. Yet at the outset there were optimists. We had beaten the Americans in the Ryder Cup at Southport a few days earlier. And with anything like luck and better judgment the result might have been different. At the conclusion no fewer than fourteen players were within five shots of the winner, and when the third round began there was a four-way tie between Leo Diegel, Syd Easterbrook, Abe Mitchell and Henry Cotton on 216, three British players apparently being in contention for the title.

To start at the beginning, the Irishman Willie Nolan set up a new record on the Old Course with a 67 which could easily have been 66 had a shot not been wasted at the Road Hole. Even so, he beat the previous best held by Bobby Jones and George Dunlap. With 71 added, Nolan took the qualifying medal. All the Americans qualified, plus Dunlap as the sole American amateur. There were two sad failures. James Braid with 88–80 – 168, and Harry Vardon 87–88 – 175 were both eliminated. Neither played like men who had previously won the title as far back as 1896 and 1901. The leader was Walter Hagen with 68, a reminder that during the previous few years he had won the title four times. One shot behind came Cyril Tolley, Ed Dudley and Tom Ferrier. Gene Sarazen was three strokes behind, Henry Cotton five along with Densmore Shute, a tall, slender American who had qualified by just one shot. Another

American, Craig Wood, returned a 77. At the end of the second day Hagen's lead had been cut to one stroke. Ed Dudley, one of the smoothest swingers in the US team, took second place with 71 and 70. Abe Mitchell kept home hopes alive with a splendid 68 which included a five at the eighteenth. The defending champion, Gene Sarazen, looked a threat until trouble in Hell's Bunker at the fourteenth upset his card.

On the final day, a strong wind made the homeward half tough going. Even so, there were some massive drives aided by the hard ground. At the Long Hole Out, Craig Wood drove some 430 yards to finish in a bunker in front of the green. On other holes the wind took its toll. Scores reflected dashed hopes. Hagen faded with 79 and 82 to finish nineteenth. He collected a seven at the fourteenth. Sarazen took eight at the fourteenth, Easterbrook seven. Sarazen could have won but took six at the eleventh. He still managed a 73. Leo Diegel almost had his hands on the trophy. On the last green, he needed a long putt to win, which he missed, then a short one to tie, and again he missed. While all this was happening, the man in the driving-seat was Denny Shute. Relentlessly consistent, he produced four rounds of 73. There were no fireworks, just business-like shot-making that produced regular figures. This son of a Scottish-born professional, Herman Shute, had been brought up not far from St Andrews and certainly enjoyed his homecoming. His nearest challenger was Craig Wood. On the fifteenth tee a finish of 4–4–5–4 would have won. Once again the fourteenth took its toll – six meant the last three holes had to be done in par. He did just that and nearly reached the home green with a massive drive. In the 36-hole playoff, Wood had a disastrous start. He put his second into the Swilcan burn at the first and needed six to Shute's four. At the second hole Wood hooked his approach into a bunker, needed three putts and was four shots behind Shute, which became five after four holes. Then came a faltering period. Shute three-putted at the ninth and tenth. Wood carded three at the sixth. Both dithered at the eleventh, and halved in double-bogey fives. At the fourteenth, the margin had been cut to two strokes, but the round ended with Shute on 75 to 78. The second round saw Shute in a commanding position. With four holes left, he was seven strokes ahead, eventually finishing with a 74 to win by five shots. Densmore Shute was a worthy winner, a victory that must have compensated for the missed putt at Southport which lost the Ryder Cup. From the British point of view, the playoff was more an exhibition than a decider, but nothing could detract from the consistent excellence of Shute's shot-making throughout the Championship. If he was not given to extrovert excitement after winning the title, nothing concealed the sheer joy expressed by his wife Patsy.

The old stone bridge over the Swilcan Burn.

Allan Robertson — over a century
ago the only ball-maker in St Andrews
with Tom Morris and Lang Willie as
assistants.

A portrait of Tom Morris by
Sir George Reid.

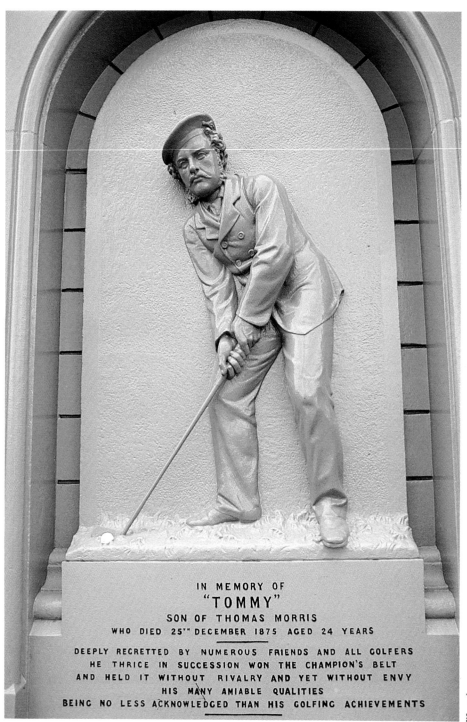

IN MEMORY OF
"TOMMY"
SON OF THOMAS MORRIS
WHO DIED 25TH DECEMBER 1875 AGED 24 YEARS

DEEPLY REGRETTED BY NUMEROUS FRIENDS AND ALL GOLFERS
HE THRICE IN SUCCESSION WON THE CHAMPION'S BELT
AND HELD IT WITHOUT RIVALRY AND YET WITHOUT ENVY
HIS MANY AMIABLE QUALITIES
BEING NO LESS ACKNOWLEDGED THAN HIS GOLFING ACHIEVEMENTS

The grave of young Tom Morris in the Cathedral
grounds. The sculptor was John Rhind of Edinburgh.

Play-off Figures

First Round:

Shute	4–4–4–4–4–4–5–4–3 – 36
Wood	6–6–4–5–4–3–5–3–3 – 39
Shute	4–5–4–5–4–4–4–5–4 – 39 – 75
Wood	4–5–4–4–5–5–4–4–4 – 39 – 78

Second Round:

Shute	4–4–4–5–4–4–4–3–4 – 36
Wood	4–5–4–4–4–4–6–4–4 – 39
Shute	3–3–5–4–5–5–4–5–4 – 38 – 74 – 149
Wood	3–4–4–5–4–4–4–5–4 – 37 – 76 – 154

Densmore Shute (USA)	73–73–73–73 – 292
play-off	75–74 – 149
Craig Wood (USA)	77–72–68–75 – 292
play-off	78–76 – 154
Gene Sarazen (USA)	72–73–73–75 – 293
Leo Diegel (USA)	75–70–71–77 – 293
Syd Easterbrook (England)	73–72–71–77 – 293
Olin Dutra (USA)	76–76–70–72 – 294
Abe Mitchell (England)	74–68–74–78 – 294

Densmore Shute took the Open trophy back to America in 1933.

Hector Thomson
1936

In 1936, the possibility that Lawson Little would win the Amateur Championship for the third successive year was avoided through the all-conquering American joining the professional ranks. For two years he had dominated the amateur scene on both sides of the Atlantic. In 1934, he beat D. Goldman for the US Amateur Championship by 8 and 7 and repeated the feat against W. Emery the following season by 4 and 2. At Prestwick in 1934, he had annihilated James Wallace by 14 and 13, then narrowly beaten Dr Tweddell by one hole in a David and Goliath final at Lytham. Now the field was possibly open for a home victory because the American invasion at St Andrews was token. Their absence was barely noticed amid the exciting golf that week. Cyril Tolley had an epic match against G. A. Hill. The quality of the golf was excellent. Hill stood three up on the fifteenth tee after an inspired spell of shot-making. The fifteenth went to Tolley in a three. He added the sixteenth, and halved the Road Hole in five to become dormy. A typical Tolley drive produced a winning four as Hill three-putted, which meant extra holes. Luck ran out for Tolley. He was stymied and Hill won the day.

The clash between Bob Sweeny and Jack McLean was another cliff-hanger. At the outset, the American had the edge and went four up with five to play, but lost the fourteenth and fifteenth and three-putted the seventeenth and eighteenth. The nineteenth was halved, but Sweeny sank a six-footer for the match on the twentieth. The dark horse of the championship was Jim Ferrier, a powerful Australian who looked a natural successor to Lawson Little. Progress had been straightforward until he met Sweeny. Long driving was the order of the day. At the twelfth Ferrier exceeded 350 yards from the tee and over-drove the 316-yard sixteenth. Extra holes were

106

needed, but at the third the Australian sank a deciding putt for a birdie. The final between Hector Thomson, son of a professional and local favourite, and Jim Ferrier was played on a typical dour St Andrews day, grey with a cold northerly wind and soaking rain. The morning round ended all square after the Scot, three down, had rallied to win three holes in succession. In the afternoon Thomson's short but accurate golf gave him a two-hole lead at the turn which was reduced to one at the eleventh, but he recovered the two-hole margin at the fourteenth. He came to the seventeenth tee two up with two to play. The Australian won the Road Hole in 4 to 5. The climax came at the last hole where Thomson played the shot of a lifetime. His second finished inches from the hole for an eagle two. Ferrier sportingly conceded, picked up his opponent's ball, and congratulated him on what had been a superb victory. Almost throughout, Thomson had to play the odd which put pressure on the Australian's precision shots. It was a widely acclaimed home victory, with Scotland and St Andrews taking the honours.

Left:
Hector Thomson played the golf of his life when he beat Jim Ferrier of Australia at the 36th in the 1936 Amateur Championship.

Right:
Jim Ferrier, whose power game threatened to be too strong for the Scot, Thomson.

Richard Burton
1939

The 1939 Open Championship produced a glut of consistent golf, several upsets, a potential American threat, amateur brilliance and an Open Champion who raised his game at the critical moment. On the Old and New Courses, 254 players tackled the two qualifying rounds. The opening day saw James Bruen and Lawson Little equal the amateur record of 69 held by Bobby Jones. Percy Alliss, father of the golf-chatterer on television, carded the New Course in 69. On the second day, Bruen added a second 69 to lead the qualifiers, with Henry Cotton and Lawson Little bracketed together on 142. Everything changed in the first round proper. Wind, rain and sleet hardly helped. Even when the weather improved, the Old Course set a severe examination. Martin Pose, the Argentinian, had a language problem. Not understanding the rules, he grounded his club on the grass beneath the wall at the seventeenth and incurred a two-stroke penalty. The fourteenth was costly for Little, while Bobby Locke needed eight and seven in the first two rounds, a blow to his pride, for he ruefully said afterwards that in four years of championship golf he had never had six on a card.

Johnny Bulla was the real surprise. This powerful, comparatively unknown golfer from Chicago had problems before the Open began. His putter had to be discarded because it did not conform to Royal and Ancient requirements, and he was committed to use a cheap drugstore ball. Under the circumstances it was hardly surprising that his opening round was 77, but he made amends with three rounds of 71–71–73. That was the target to beat. Bill Shankland, the burly Australian who had been a professional Rugby player, should have done so. On the home green he had to sink a longish putt to tie with Bulla; he missed and did the same with the return. Johnny Fallon had 71–73–71 but finished with a disastrous 79. Alfred Perry, Reginald Whitcombe, the defending champion, and Sam King threw away their chances and finished on 294. In the end it was Dick Burton's turn. The strong, Lancashire-born professional needed 73 to tie. Out in 35 with a two at the eleventh, he found himself requiring on the fifteenth tee two fives and two fours to win by a stroke. The title almost slipped away at the sixteenth, but he sank a single putt. Five went on the card at the Road Hole after an immaculate second shot. His drive at the last almost reached the Valley of Sin. A firm run-up finished ten feet from the pin. He sank the putt for a birdie and the Championship.

Richard Burton was a worthy champion, who, because of the break caused by the war years, never reaped the financial benefits that went with the title. He missed his peak years as a player and was never again in contention for the Open title, but he made his mark as a superb golfer with an impressive tournament and Ryder Cup record.

Richard Burton	70–72–77–71 – 290
Johnny Bulla (USA)	77–71–71–73 – 292
John Fallon	71–73–71–79 – 294
Bill Shankland	72–73–72–77 – 294
Alfred Perry	71–74–73–76 – 294
Reginald Whitcombe	71–75–74–74 – 294
Sam King	74–72–75–73 – 294
Martin Pose (Argentina)	71–72–76–76 – 295
Percy Alliss	75–73–74–74 – 296

Opposite:
Richard Burton's victory in the Open coincided with the break caused by the war years.

Sam Snead
1946

The first post-war Open Championship attracted an entry of 225 and opened quietly. No records were broken. Syd Scott of Carlisle led on the Old Course with 73, followed by W. S. Collins, J. Morris and Joe Kirkwood on 74. Richard Burton, the holder, was 76. On the New Course, the Australian Norman von Nida, Reginald Whitcombe and Dai Rees were 72. Henry Cotton, Arthur Lacey, John Langley and Bobby Locke were 75. The weather was ideal. One hundred and ten survived the qualifying cut, 91 professionals and 19 amateurs. Von Nida headed the list with 73–72 – 145. Most of the invaders succeeded. Sam King failed through three-putting on seven greens. Cyril Tolley came to disaster on the New Course and tore up his card. Charles Whitcombe lost his putting touch, and Ernest Whitcombe, Arthur Lacey and Hector Thomson, who was competing in his first major tournament as a professional, failed to make the grade. Burton left himself with three shots to spare. John Panton, a young Pitlochry assistant, disqualified himself because unwittingly he had practised putting on one of the New Course greens. His second round of 77 would have qualified him comfortably.

The first round proper saw Locke take a one-shot lead from Cotton and von Nida. The South African's 69 included only one putt on seven greens;

Out: 4–4–4–4–4–4–3–3 – 34
In: 3–3–4–4–5–4–4–4 – 35 – 69

Locke's round knocked Cotton off the leader-mark, though his 70 could easily have been two strokes better. Australia shared second place, with America holding three places out of five in the third bracket of the scoreboard, a couple of shots behind the leader. Disaster at the Road Hole cost Johnny Bulla the lead. With two holes to play he was four under fours and looked set for 68, possibly 67. His second to the seventeenth went on the road. He tried to pitch off the metalled surface, but the ball struck the grass verge and came back. A fourth shot just reached the gravel pathway short of the green. The next shot sent the ball across the green but two putts saw seven marked on his card. Four at the eighteenth gave a 71 to the runner-up. Snead returned a steady 71 and was joined by the unobtrusive W. C. A. Hancock of Stockport.

Thursday was the most eventful day. We had become reconciled to the prospect of an overseas lead at the halfway stage, when Cotton played his finest fighting round since his Open victory at Carnoustie in 1937. He went out in the most troublesome weather of the day with a stiff wind on the homeward half – 35 to the turn, he started back 3–3–4. Fives crept in at the fourteenth and fifteenth, but he played one of the boldest shots of the championship at the sixteenth, placing a long iron shot a couple of yards from the pin. Then came a tense moment at the eighteenth. The ball was ten yards from the hole. The putt dropped for a three. His score of 70 put Cotton in the lead with 140. There was more cause for home satisfaction. Dai Rees returned a scorching 67. The figures speak for themselves:

Out: 4–4–3–4–4–4–3–3 – 33
In: 4–3–4–5–4–4–3–4–3 – 34 – 67

A comparison with the par score is interesting:

Out: 4–4–4–4–5–4–4–3–4 – 36
In: 4–3–4–4–5–4–4–5–4 – 37 – 73

110

Seven birdies and only one hole over the par figure was good going. The diminutive golfer was full of jaunty confidence. There was none of the grim determination and concentration of Cotton, just an overflowing of Welsh elation. Other highlights included Charles Ward holing-out in one at the short eighth. At the end of the day Snead finished second, one shot behind Cotton. Von Nida and Joe Kirkwood were three strokes behind them. Five overseas men were in the first nine. James Adams, Max Faulkner, W. J. Branch, Reg Horne, W. J. Cox and Arthur Havers failed to qualify.

The final day was a mixed bag of hopes. Locke, first out at 8 am, returned a steady 75. Cotton was in the toils and was one under fives on the eleventh tee. Ward had a businesslike 73. Bulla, out in 36, mastered the Road Hole in four and returned 72. Snead had a 74. Rees, still exuberant, went out in 37 to finish with 73. The third round ended with Snead, Bulla and Rees bracketed together at 215. Cotton was one shot behind, while Locke and Ward were close behind. The fourth round was traumatic. One of six players could win, with the odds on a tie. The breeze had freshened. Cotton began badly by finding the Swilcan with his second, and then took three putts at the next hole. Forty out was too many. Rees began with a wild drive which headed for the rails, hit a spectator and fell a couple of feet inside the course. His next shot found the burn; seven went on the card. Then came three putts at the second for a five. Twelve shots for two holes; three putts at the third – 17 for three holes and 42 to the turn. A three at the Road

Sam Snead *left* on the way to winning the 1946 Open and *right* being presented with the trophy.

Hole and four at the eighteenth for a round of 80 – aggregate 295 – put him level with Cotton and Ward, and one shot behind Locke and Bulla. The latter wasted a couple of strokes at the last two holes. He played a sound second to the Road Hole, then a poor chip, followed by three putts. He needed a four to gain the lead, but missed a tiny putt at the eighteenth to tie with the South African.

The Championship was virtually given to Snead. Provided he steered clear of disaster, routine figures would be sufficient. He played so steadily that he came to the last tee knowing a seven would tie. Four shots only were needed. Victory by a margin of four strokes. Snead's graceful swing was well-nigh flawless that week. A man of real power, the West Virginian had taken the title with a feast of brilliant shots. At the outset he took time to settle down and in the process changed caddies three times, the last carrier being rewarded with the winner's purse, then £150, at the 1946 exchange rate worth $600.

Sam Snead (USA)	71–70–74–75 – 290
Johnny Bulla (USA)	71–72–72–79 – 294
Bobby Locke (South Africa)	69–74–75–76 – 294
Henry Cotton (GB)	70–70–76–79 – 295
Dai Rees (GB)	75–67–73–80 – 295
Charles Ward (GB)	73–73–73–76 – 295
Norman von Nida (Australia)	70–76–74–75 – 295

St Andrews introduced strict measures in 1946 to control spectators. For the first time they were excluded from the playing area, an innovation which marked the beginning of the control system for all big golfing events, a method which today has gone too far.

Frank Stranahan
1950

The 1950 Amateur Championship attracted an entry of 324 which included such names as Willie Turnesa, winner of the title in 1947 and the US Amateur Championship the following year; Francis Ouimet, the 1914 US Open Champion; Cyril Tolley, the 1920 Amateur Champion; Jim McHale; Bill Campbell, another American who was later to win the US amateur title; Joe Carr, Sam McCready and the favourite, Frank Stranahan. There were plenty of highlights.

In the first round several thousand watched the fortunes of Bing Crosby against the local golfer, James Wilson, who won at the sixteenth green after a match in which the American played shots Bob Hope would have envied. Bill Campbell eliminated Willie Turnesa with an eagle three at the Road Hole only to lose to Joe Carr after an extra hole. McCready made steady progress at the expense of F. G. Dewar (5 and 4), S. B. Williamson (2 and 1), and Cecil Ewing (1 hole). Dick Chapman beat Willie Whitelaw (6 and 5), E. S. Nugent-Head (3 and 2), Jack Mitchell on the last green, and Jim McHale by a single hole in a match of fluctuating fortunes. The favourite, Frank Stranahan, accounted for A. C. Gibson in ten holes, risked defeat against Bob Neill but scrambled home on the home green, and beat Cyril Tolley in the semi-final after a fine performance by the Englishman who had won the title three years before his opponent was born. The all-American final was disappointing, with somewhat indifferent golf. The weather did not help with cold wind and rain. Stranahan led

Opposite: A jubilant Frank Stranahan after winning the Amateur Championship for the second time when he beat fellow countryman Richard Chapman on the 30th green.

Chapman at lunch by three up then took five of the next twelve to clinch the match on the 30th green and become Amateur Champion for the second time.

An accurate pen-portrait of Frank Stranahan at that time was not easy. Admired by many, criticised by others, censured by a few, the young American had the self-assurance of a veteran, sauntering with supreme indifference through life with a golf club in his hand. Few people in Britain really knew Stranahan. I did not profess to understand his extraordinary devotion to the game. I have never seen any man spend so many hours, day after day, hitting golf balls into space. There was obviously some inner urge which would neither be stilled nor satisfied until the goal was reached. What that target was only Stranahan could say. I believe Bobby Jones achieved what Frank would like to have done, namely to win the four major golfing titles in the same year. Such inspiration did not really concern us. That was his business as a golfer. In the same way that the plumber's thoughts are no business of ours until he translates them into terms of pipes, so Stranahan's golf affected us only on the course.

He was an extraordinary golfer to study and analyse. The swing was so regimented that it bordered upon that of an automaton. I liked Stranahan. I admired his single-mindedness, though I could not understand it. His success did not consist of the sum total of the shots he made in a year, for, whatever the sage might have said, genius is not an affair of accountancy. It is the unique ability to concentrate on a subject to the exclusion of everything else. The snide remarks made about the American were unjustified. Labels have a habit of becoming libels. An instance of this occurred at St Andrews in 1950. After winning the Amateur Championship, Stranahan received the trophy from Lord Balfour, then quietly withdrew from the scene. Normally Rusacks Hotel would have been the centre of celebration. The absence of anything of that nature led to speculation and later to assertion. None of these was true. That evening I sat down at a small dinner-party held in a quiet Lundin Links hotel. There were eight of us. The trophy was on a side-table. Stranahan's caddie was the outside visitor. He appeared for a few minutes with his parents, who wanted to see the trophy and meet 'his' man. The rest of the evening was restful, the only interruption being a transatlantic congratulatory call from Stranahan senior. The party broke up at 11.00 pm.

That evening reflected a side of Frank Stranahan's nature which few people saw. He was essentially quiet to the point of modesty, taking delight in pleasures that cynics would have called simple, if not naïve. The old Yorkshire proverb is so true: 'There are trimmings for all kinds of cloth, and buttons for fustian.' It applies with equal meaning to things of the spirit. No one can tell what makes life pleasanter for the individual.

Opposite:
This frozen action study of Frank Stranahan shows a copybook back-swing made possible by the American's physical fitness.

Peter Thomson
1955

We tend to forget the domination exercised by Peter Thomson in the Open Championship. For eight years it became anyone's guess who would be runner-up. He was three times. On the other five occasions he claimed the title. Instead of a rough-tongued, aggressive Australian approach, Thomson played and won as if he enjoyed every shot. That image was not far out. It was the way he tackled the Old Course which he ranked as the best course in the world. His record at St Andrews speaks for itself. There was every cause for satisfaction.

The 1954 *News of the World* match-play championship reflected his buoyant approach. In the fourth round he was two down with two to play against John Panton, but he struck back with an eagle at the Road Hole, followed by a birdie three at the eighteenth and sank a long winning putt at the twenty-second. In the next round a close fight with Bobby Locke ended on the last hole. His opponent in the final was a determined Johnny Fallon who refused to be the underdog. He matched Thomson shot for shot. It was 34 holes before the Australian squared the match and then took the deciding hole at the 38th.

For St Andrews 1955 was a special year. Thomson arrived as defending champion after his Birkdale win in 1954. Three hundred competitors had entered, including Ed Furgol, Byron Nelson, Frank Stranahan, Bobby Locke, Antonio Cerda and Kel Nagle, but the greatest threat came from an unexpected quarter. A comparatively unknown Yorkshire professional, Frank Jowle, set the pace in the qualifying round. On the New Course he carded a sensational 63 – 30 out, 33 home – eight under par, to beat the existing record by six strokes. Six threes from the start and only 29 putts gave a hint of what he could produce, but it was Eric Brown who shared the

115

first round lead of 69 with Syd Scott and Dai Rees. Thomson returned 71. By the end of the second round he led with Brown on 139, and went into lunch on the final day still holding a one-shot lead over Jowle with Harry Weetman and Bobby Locke close behind. In the last round the Australian faltered with a six at the fifth and seven at the fourteenth, while Fallon with an outward half of 31 had pulled back four shots, but wilted under the pressure. An inward half of 39 for 70 and an aggregate of 283 left Thomson the winner by two strokes. He was the fifth golfer to have won the Open two years in succession and the 281 was the lowest aggregate in an Open at St Andrews, beating Bobby Jones's 1927 record by four shots.

Peter Thomson was the model of correctness and is remembered as the professional golfer par excellence. He reflected orthodoxy at its best and was the ideal model on which to base an uncomplicated style.

P. W. Thomson (Australia)	71–68–70–72 – 281
J. Fallon (Huddersfield)	73–67–73–70 – 283
F. Jowle (Edgbaston)	70–71–69–74 – 284
A. D. Locke (S. Africa)	74–69–70–72 – 285
A. Cerda (Argentina)	73–71–71–71 – 286

Peter Thomson of Australia, immediately after winning the 1955 Open.

Bobby Locke
1957

Bobby Locke came to St Andrews in 1957 with a proud record in the Open Championship. Winner at Sandwich in 1949, at Troon in 1950 and again victorious at Lytham in 1952, the chances of his recording a fourth win to put himself alongside James Braid, who did just that in 1909, were improved by the comparatively weak American entry. The main threat came from Cary Middlecoff and Frank Stranahan, who led a group of ten, but main opposition was expected to come from Peter Thomson, the Australian who also had triple Open wins at Birkdale 1954, St Andrews 1955 and Hoylake 1956. British hopes centred on Henry Cotton, Max Faulkner and Eric Brown.

At the end of the qualifying rounds, the list was headed by Locke who was bracketed alongside Bernard Hunt on 137, but in the championship proper the pace was set by Eric Brown and Laurie Ayton with 67s. The former had not always sung the praises of the Old Course, but this time he found the going to his liking and carded the outward half in 30, which included seven threes. Two more followed but a six at the thirteenth prevented the round from becoming a pace-setter. It was Ayton, very much on home territory, who matched it with 34 out and an inward half of 3–2–4–4–5–4–3–4–4. The young Australian, Bruce Crampton, finished in 68, one shot ahead of Locke. Cary Middlecoff did not impress with 72, nor Stranahan with 74, but both improved with 71s in the second round. Eric Brown led at the halfway stage with 67–72. Ayton dropped back with 76. A surprise challenge came from Flory van Donck, of Belgium, who finished one stroke behind Brown. Locke was 141, Thomson 142. The final two rounds increased the pressures. Cary Middlecoff trailed on 289. Crampton faded with 298. Brown had useful

Bobby Locke, after winning the 1957 Open — his fourth Championship in nine years, entertained the crowd with a Scottish song.

rounds of 73 and 71 but they were not good enough to contain either Locke or Thomson. The South African returned a third round of 68 which the Australian might have matched had shots not been dropped on the outward half. Tom Haliburton came strongly into the lists with a third round of 68, but fell away in the final effort after lunch. Locke did not weaken – 70 gave an aggregate of 279 to equal the lowest Open total which he had established at Troon five years earlier. Thomson's challenge was keen. He matched the South African almost shot for shot, but went out in 34. Each had a last round of 70, but it was two shots too many for Thomson. Both these players had destroyed the former American domination of the Open, substituting instead a Commonwealth monopoly. This time it was the portly Bobby Locke in the inevitable plus-fours, white cap and white shoes whose effortless shot-making had brought Open victory for the fourth time, an orthodox stylist who could be copied with impunity. He had earned the reputation of being one of the greatest putters in the world. His ability to read greens was almost uncanny. The thoroughness of his preparation was such that it was difficult to imagine a putt being missed. He had the knack of reading any green. Few golfers were so meticulous in routine checks on the line. Once his mind was made up, the South African played the putt with a rhythmic ease that was the envy of all golfers. It was certainly true at St Andrews.

A. D. Locke	69–72–68–70 – 279
P. W. Thomson	73–69–70–70 – 282
E. C. Brown	67–72–73–71 – 283
A. Miguel	72–72–69–72 – 285
D. C. Thomas	72–74–70–70 – 286
T. B. Haliburton	72–73–68–73 – 286
W. D. Smith (amateur)	71–72–72–71 – 286
F. van Donck	72–68–74–72 – 286

Joe Carr
1958

The Old Course was in a grey, harsh mood for the 1958 Amateur Championship, as many entrants found to their cost, but spectators who stoically trudged after the players were rewarded by several superb matches. The semi-final between Joe Carr and Michael Bonallack produced a rare scrap. The Englishman went out in 33 to be two up, but Carr struck back on the homeward half, when 36 was sufficient to turn the deficit into a lead of two holes. After lunch Carr maintained the pressure to finish the winner by 3 and 2. In the final, Alan Thirwell took advantage of lapses on the greens by the Irishman to be four up at the seventh, but the weakness disappeared. The putter began to work and the lead was whittled down. All square at the sixteenth and a birdie at the eighteenth meant Carr went into the clubhouse one up. The pressure continued in the afternoon. By the fifth the lead for Carr was three holes. Thirwell won the seventh with a birdie and halved the next three holes. The turning-point was the twelfth, where Carr followed a massive drive by sinking an enormous putt for a two. The next four holes were halved in pars, and the Amateur title was Joe Carr's for the second time. In 1953 he beat Harvie Ward at Hoylake by two holes. This time the margin was 3 and 2.

Joe Carr was such a seasoned campaigner that the public automatically expected him to do well. They were not disappointed at St Andrews. On form, he was capable of winning any championship. He did not suffer from an inferiority complex, and was unimpressed by the records of his colleagues. What they could do, he could do better. This belief in his own ability, which was not misplaced, was always a goad, the stepping-stone to further success, as happened two years later at Portrush, this time by a margin of 8 and 7.

Joe Carr, exuberant and fluent striker of the ball.

Kel Nagle
1960

So perverse is human nature that special occasions, long anticipated, often become something of an anti-climax. That might have happened when the Centenary Open Championship was staged at St Andrews in 1960. It could have been self-consciously pompous. Instead the golf was left to speak for itself. It was perhaps slightly disappointing that the entry did not include a stronger American contingent, but the quality was there in the person of Arnold Palmer, fresh from winning the US Open at Cherry Hills Country Club in Denver, Colorado, with a crushing final round of 65 that gave him victory by two shots over Jack Nicklaus, Ben Hogan and Julius Boros. The St Andrews field also included Gary Player, Roberto de Vicenzo, Peter Thomson, Kel Nagle, Harold Henning, with the home challenge headed by Harry Weetman, Dai Rees, Syd Scott, Eric Brown and Bernard Hunt. Whoever won would know he had been in a fight, and so it proved.

From start to finish the event was packed with incident. It began in the qualifying rounds when the veteran Gene Sarazen, the pocket Hercules of golf who was likened to the Cheshire Cat because of his expansive smile, showed he could still grin by claiming the qualifying medal with rounds of 69 and 72. At 58 he showed scant respect for the Old Course, but it was Roberto de Vicenzo who set the pace in the blustery conditions of the first round with a card of 67 – 32 out: 35 home. Another Argentinian, Fidel de Luca, came next with 69 with Kel Nagle of Australia, while Arnold Palmer shared 70 with Ken Bousfield, Peter Shanks and amateur David Blair. Gary Player, Peter Thomson and Joe Carr were bracketed together on 72s.

Arnold Palmer could with luck have been several shots better for putts rimmed the cup at the fourth, sixth,

seventh, eighth and twelfth, plus three putts at the seventeenth. De Vicenzo did not weaken in the second round and returned another 67. Nagle matched the round to stay two shots behind the leader. Palmer faltered by his standards with 71 and was seven shots adrift. Peter Thomson shot 69 to tie with Palmer, whilst Sebastian Miguel of Spain broke loose with a 68. Once again Palmer was frustrated on the greens, lipping the cup six times and again three-putting at the Road Hole.

Pressure from television caused a break with tradition. Instead of two rounds on the final day, the Championship now had four rounds over four days. Palmer made his challenge with a 70 and a total of 211, but still could not improve on five at the seventeenth. De Vicenzo returned 75 for 209 and lost his lead to Nagle, whose 71 and 207 meant a two stroke buffer. Syd Scott, so often underestimated, came good with 67 and tied with Palmer. Joe Carr equalled it, but Player and Thomson sank back with 75s.

The final day was packed with drama. With nine holes left it had become a three-cornered fight between Nagle, de Vicenzo and Palmer. All three were out in 34. Vicenzo faltered at the eleventh and failed to get a three. Palmer chopped Nagle's lead to three shots with a three at the thirteenth. Nagle tempted disaster at the fourteenth when his drive flirted with that minefield of bunkers, the Beardies, but still got his five. Three putts at the fifteenth cut his lead to two. Palmer had four at the Road Hole followed by a birdie three at the eighteenth. With Palmer playing ahead of Nagle, the Australian knew by the cheers that his 10-footer at the seventeenth had to be sunk. With no sign of nervous tension, he struck the ball into the middle of the cup. Nagle's drive at the eighteenth was shorter than Palmers, just past Granny Clark's Wynd, but pitched up to three feet short of the hole. Two putts to claim the Centenary Open. The first putt was jabbed and finished nine inches short of the hole. He made no mistake with the next. Nagle had won the title by one stroke and set up a new Championship record at St Andrews, beating Bobby Locke's 1957 aggregate of 279 by one shot.

Kel Nagle must still look at the handsome Centenary Open replica trophy and recall those four days when he won in such brilliant fashion. Australia is fortunate to have had such an admirable ambassador.

K. D. G. Nagle (Australia)	69–67–71–71 – 278
A. Palmer (USA)	70–71–70–68 – 279
B. J. Hunt (Hartsbourne)	72–73–71–66 – 282
H. R. Henning (South Africa)	72–72–69–69 – 282
R. de Vicenzo (Argentina)	67–67–75–73 – 282

Left:
To mark the Centenary Open Championship, the winner, Kel Nagle, was presented with a special replica of the trophy.

Michael Lunt
1963

Michael Lunt killed a jinx in 1963 which had pursued British amateur golf for some 37 years. Every time since 1926 that the full strength of an American Walker Cup team had entered for the Amateur Championship, the trophy had crossed the Atlantic in their luggage. Everything suggested a repetition. Not only was the US Walker Cup side there in strength, but thirty other Americans had made the trip and none of them was a push-over. The presence of Richard Davies, the American Amateur champion, and Labron Harris, the previous holder, underlined the quality of the opposition. Titles are not won on paper. Only four Americans survived to the fifth round. The quartet was Ronald Luceti, Edgar Updegraff, R. H. Sikes and Richard Davies. The last had lived dangerously. John Wilson was beaten only at the nineteenth. John Beharrell, four up at the eleventh, failed to take his chances and had to face a barrage of ruthless golf from Davies who won five holes on the homeward route, ending on the home green where Beharrell missed a vital three-foot putt.

Ronald Shade went down to Updegraff 3 and 2. Joe Carr lost to Peter Green by the same margin. In the meantime, Michael Lunt made steady progress with sturdy shot-making. He had the better of Davies by the narrow margin of one hole. Sikes went down to Updegraff 2 and 1, who went on to play Lunt. In many ways the match was a cliff-hanger, but took a definite turn when the American was three down on the sixteenth tee. He won the sixteenth and seventeenth, but Lunt had a winning four at the last hole. John Blackwell and Ron Luceti had an adventurous semi-final with patchy golf. The Englishman won the fourteenth with seven against eight and eventually the match by 3 and 2.

In the final between Blackwell and Lunt the players

Michael Lunt, who won the Amateur Championship in 1963 against the full strength of the American Walker Cup Team.

were even after the first round, Lunt needing a seven at the difficult fourteenth. The issue was still close after lunch. Blackwell won the opening hole in three to four, but lost the next five to four. The next four holes were halved. Three at the seventh put Lunt in the lead, which increased to two up at the ninth. The fourteenth again set problems Lunt could not master when he picked up, but he regained the two-hole margin at the fifteenth. Halves at the sixteenth and Road Hole saw Michael Lunt a worthy champion by 2 and 1.

Tony Lema
1964

Tony Lema has been described as a mini-carbon-copy of Walter Hagen. There were certainly similarities. Lema was ambitious, at times extrovert, but seemed self-consciously contrived when compared with the spontaneous showmanship of the Haig. Nevertheless, Lema was immensely popular with the crowds. Success had not been easy. His father, a labourer of Portuguese extraction, died when he was three, leaving the penniless mother to cope with four young children in the industrial slums of Oakland, California. Tony was a typical boy of that background. Truant from school, anything to earn the odd dollar, including caddying at the municipal course. He worked as a bottle-washer in San Francisco, served two years in the Marines in Korea, then took a job as an assistant golf professional. An uncontrolled temper did not help. Once that was mastered, he made progress, but was still an also-ran. The turning-point came when after he had failed to qualify for the 1961 American Open, Horton Smith in Detroit ironed out his putting faults. Confidence on the green produced results. Two years later, Lema won his first title in the Orange County Open Championship after a play-off with Bob Rosburg.

When Lema arrived at St Andrews in 1964 he had won four of the last five tournaments in the United States and was riding the crest of the wave, but had still to gain a major championship. He left it late. There was time for only two practice rounds on the Old Course and, even with Tip Anderson as caddie, the odds were against him with a field of 327, including such men as Jack Nicklaus, Peter Thomson, Gary Player, Bob Charles, and

Tony Lema, extrovert professional in the mould of Walter Hagen.

123

Roberto de Vicenzo. The weather did little to help. Gale-force wind left over half the entry with scores in the 80s. Peter Thomson and Bob Charles had 79. Nicklaus drove the last green with the wind behind in a round of 76. Christy O'Connor and Jean Garaialde shared the lead on 71. Lema returned 73. The second day was calmer. Nicklaus had a round of 74 which included 40 putts. Lema played superbly for a four under par 68 which put him in the lead by two shots. On the last day Nicklaus looked out of the chase, trailing Lema by nine strokes, but he struck a purple patch, highlighted on the twelfth where he sank a 60-foot putt for three to be five under par. Tension had caught up with Lema. His nine-shot lead had shrunk to two. Nicklaus went into lunch with a six under par 66.

In the final round it was Nicklaus who faltered at the fourth and the fifth, but rallied strongly with 3–4–2–3 to be out in 34. Lema responded with 4–3–3–3–4–3 to equal the 34. Nicklaus added another 34 for the inward half.

A. Lema (USA)	73–68–68–70 – 279
J. Nicklaus (USA)	76–74–66–68 – 284
R. de Vicenzo (Argentina)	76–72–70–67 – 285
B. J. Hunt (Hartsbourne)	73–74–70–70 – 287
B. Devlin (Australia)	72–72–73–73 – 290

His aggregate of 284 meant that on the tenth tee Lema had a seven-shot lead. Apart from hiccups at the twelfth, fourteenth and seventeenth, Lema was in a safe position at the home hole. Only a disaster could snatch the title. A useful drive left him 80 yards short with the Valley of Sin to clear. Lema played an old-fashioned, Scottish invented run-up to four feet short of the pin, sank the putt for a birdie and became Open Champion by a margin of five strokes, a win worthy of a true champion. Tragically, Tony and his wife died in an air crash on the way to a tournament in America. He is remembered as an amiable young man whose graceful swing and determination earned true reward at St Andrews.

'Mary Queen of Scots appears to have practised this game, for it was made a charge against her by her enemies, as an instance of her indifference to Darnley's fate, that she was seen playing at golf and pall-mall in the fields beside Seton, a few days after his death.'

Inventories of Mary Queen of Scots, 1863

Jack Nicklaus
1970 and 1978

Every Open Championship has its quota of memorable moments; 1970 was no exception and ended in dramatic fashion. Tony Jacklin set the ball rolling in the first round by reeling off a string of remarkable figures. The start of 3–3–3 set the pattern for an outward half of 29 which included an eagle two at the ninth when he holed out a wedge shot. The purple patch continued, but the Old Course was spared embarrassment when the heavens opened, torrential rain flooded the course and play was suspended with the scores already in counting. Balls were left where they were overnight. Unfortunately when play resumed the next day the Jacklin magic was missing – 4–5–5–4 meant a round of 67 instead of an all-time record.

When the first round eventually ended, there were several surprises. Neil Coles had roused himself to return a card of 65, one shot better than Tommy Horton, with Maurice Bembridge, John Richardson, Florentino Molino of the Argentine and Harold Henning on the 67 mark. Lee Trevino, Arnold Palmer, Jack Nicklaus and Doug Sanders were bunched together at 68. In the second round, Coles tailed off with a 74. Jacklin's 70 gave him 137, one stroke behind Trevino, who shared the lead with Nicklaus and Sanders. Nicklaus's round was helped by a massive drive of over 300 yards at the twelfth followed by a fifteen-foot putt for an eagle. The big surprise was Doug Sanders. The 37-year-old professional from Georgia had not been considered as a serious contender. For three years he had failed to figure in the winner's lists and had been obliged to compete in the

Jack Nicklaus won the 1970 Open through Doug Sanders' tragic error on the 18th green.

126

qualifying rounds for the Open, returning 67 and 74 over the Panmure course. Against that, Sanders had finished second to Nicklaus in the 1966 Open at Muirfield, so was used to playing under pressure.

Conditions for the third round were frightful, with wind and rain sweeping across the course. Trevino maintained his lead of two shots over Sanders, Nicklaus and Jacklin. Conditions were even worse on the last day. The issue became a duel between Nicklaus and Sanders. Nicklaus began to falter on the greens. Sanders found his touch. Everything turned on the last two holes. Nicklaus played the Road Hole brilliantly but had to settle for par, one stroke behind Sanders. At the eighteenth Nicklaus struck an overstrong uphill putt from the Valley of Sin and saw the ball finish twenty feet past the hole. Sanders needed pars at the seventeenth and eighteenth for victory by one shot. The Road Hole was almost disastrous. The second shot was bunkered, but he recovered to a couple of feet from the hole and saved his par. That left par four at the last for the title. The drive was well placed, but the second was overstrong. Two putts to win. The first putt finished about a foot from the hole. Sanders took his time. He was so near to victory. The ball just failed to drop and his chance had slipped away. The playoff was very close. In the end Jack Nicklaus became champion by a single shot, 72 to 73, with his birdie three at the last hole deciding the issue. For Doug Sanders it was a cruel end to a wonderful fight, the ambition of a lifetime missed by less than two feet.

| J. Nicklaus (USA) | 68–69–73–73 – 283 |
| D. Sanders (USA) | 68–71–71–73 – 283 |

Playoff:
| Nicklaus | 72 |
| Sanders | 73 |

H. Henning (South Africa)	67–72–73–73 – 285
L. Trevino (USA)	68–68–72–77 – 285
A. Jacklin (GB)	67–70–73–76 – 286
N. C. Coles (GB)	65–74–72–76 – 287
P. A. Oosterhuis (GB)	73–69–69–76 – 287

A group photograph of past Open Champions, taken at the 1970 Open. *Back row:* A.G. Havers, G. Sarazen, R. Burton, F. Daly, R. De Vicenzo, A. Palmer, K. Nagle, B. Locke, H. Cotton, P.W. Thomson. *Front row:* D. Shute, R.J. Charles, M. Faulkner, J. Nicklaus, T. Jacklin, G. Player.

Richard Siderowf
1976

In 1976 the Amateur championship trophy went back to America in the luggage of Richard Siderowf, the US Walker Cup veteran, 1971 Canadian Amateur champion and previous winner of the British Amateur title in 1972, when he beat Peter Moody at Porthcawl by 5 and 3. This time Siderowf was opposed by the experienced John Davies. A shared result would have been fairer, for neither deserved to lose. In the end the American took the title at the 37th. Siderowf is remembered for the crispness and lazy deliberation of his long iron shots. His approach to the game was both methodical and tireless. He mirrored the traditional American will to win and had the guts to overcome not only a tough opponent but the wiles of the Old Course. He was the type of champion that St Andreans respect.

Richard Siderowf took the Amateur title back to the States in 1976.

The Open won by the Old Course

The weather for the 1978 Open Championship was ideal for low scoring. There had been sufficient rain to tame the fairways and leave the greens with responsive surfaces. For four days the conditions could not be faulted. Everyone was prepared for the Old Course to be taken apart by the power golf of the world's greatest players. Not only was the Open Championship at stake, but the very reputation of the Old Course was at risk. In the end an American took the title, but it was the famous links that won the Championship. Time and again its wiles and traps destroyed hopes and dented egos. Two holes in particular lived up to their sinister reputations. The fourteenth or Long Hole In took its toll of Lanny Wadkins. In the first round he seemed set for a useful round of about 69 when he drove out-of-bounds twice and finished with an eight on the card. In the second round he did the same and that was that. Both Arnold Palmer and Brian Barnes chalked-up sixes. Even Jack Nicklaus faltered when he drove into the Beardies.

The real villain of the round was the Road Hole. In sadistic fashion it spoilt innumerable cards. Brian Barnes looked as though at long last he was going to challenge for the title. He came to the seventeenth in the first round with a useful score of three under par with a probable four at the Road Hole. It was wishful thinking. His putt finished in a bunker and a six resulted. Arnold Palmer was rejuvenated. After 71 in the first round, he stood four under for the Championship on the seventeenth tee. His drive met trouble and he was lucky to get away with a seven. The same mistake was repeated in

The natural flowing action of Jack Nicklaus's swing brings the body round in fluent fashion.

Past champions line up at the 1978 Open. *Back row:* Robert de Vicenzo, Peter Thomson, Bob Charles, Arnold Palmer, Johnny Miller, Tom Weiskopf, Jack Nicklaus, Bobby Locke. *Front row:* Max Faulkner, Fred Daly, Tony Jacklin, Henry Cotton, W. Muirhead (Captain, R & A), Tom Watson, Gary Player, Kel Nagle.

the third round and gone were his chances. Severiano Ballesteros was another to suffer at this hole. Having a 69 in the first round, then out in 33, he was looking good when a sliced drive at the Road Hole meant a six and a lost opportunity of leading the field. Even worse was the experience of Tsuneyuki Nakajima of Japan, who was playing steadily with 70–71 when disaster came in the third round at the Road Hole. His third shot, a putt of some 25 yards, finished up in a bunker. Recovery shots were embarrassing. The ball remained in the sand until eventually he escaped with a nine.

The Road Hole lived up to its dreaded reputation. It is a par four, measuring 461 yards, but on that first day not one of the 154 players managed a birdie, and only about twenty managed the par.

The final day the Old Course revealed different problems because the wind had veered completely. The second hole showed the difference. Instead of a wedge for the second shot, a three-wood was needed. Only the strategic players coped with the change. Everything pointed to a close finish, with ten players within three shots of the three leaders, Isao Aoki, Ben Crenshaw and Severiano Ballesteros on 139. Those who failed to make the cut at 148 included such names as Graham Marsh, Johnny Miller, Lanny Wadkins, Bob Charles, Tony Jacklin and Ed Sneed. Of those challenging, Jack Nicklaus was favourite, but a stirring challenge was made by Simon Owen who refused to be intimidated. Partnered with Nicklaus, he went out in 37, birdied the tenth, twelfth and fourteenth and was bracketed with Nicklaus at six under par. At the fifteenth he hooked his drive, failed to find the green with his second, but holed his 30-yard chip for a three to take the lead at seven under. Nicklaus took it back at the next hole with a three and added a four at the seventeenth, where Owen finished on the road and needed five. Everything turned on the last hole. Nicklaus made no mistake. Left with two for the Championship, he duly obliged and became Champion again. By his victory he became the first to win four major titles three times or more, three US Opens, five Masters, four American PGA Championships, three Opens and two US Amateur titles. Eight years had passed since Nicklaus had beaten Doug Sanders in a playoff at St Andrews. This time too he had earned success the hard way, culminating on the last green. Jack Nicklaus had taken the title, but in the end it was the Old Course that won the Championship by refusing to be taken apart by the players. They still had a great deal to learn from the most famous links in the world.

J. Nicklaus (USA)	71–72–69–69 – 281
S. Owen (New Zealand)	70–75–67–71 – 283
B. Crenshaw (USA)	70–69–73–71 – 283
R. Floyd (USA)	69–75–71–68 – 283
T. Kite (USA)	72–69–72–70 – 283
P. Oosterhuis (GB)	72–70–69–73 – 284

Philippe Ploujoux
1981

The 1981 Amateur Championship attracted an entry rich in national talent which produced a series of tense matches. The field included Jesus Lopez, a young Spaniard of immense potential; Francois Illouz, who had just won the French Open Amateur Championship; Canada was represented by Douglas Roxburgh; the previous season's beaten finalist, David Suddards from South Africa; an Australian, Tony Gresham; Wayne Player, son of Gary. The home entry was not short of talent with Ronan Rafferty, Philip Walton, Paul Way, Michael McLean, Duncan Evans the defending champion, Peter McEvoy, Amateur champion of 1977 and 1978, Peter Deeble the English champion, Roger Chapman, Geoffrey Green and Ian Hutcheon. Trying to name the winner before play began was like predicting what would win the Grand National.

At the end of the first day many such bets had crashed. Ian Hutcheon lost to the Australian Gerard Power after an untidy match. Richard Siderowf, the veteran US Walker Cup player who had won the title on the Old Course five years earlier, lost to John Huggan, a Scottish youth international, who began the demolition job by sinking a 25-yard chip at the third for a birdie, and went two up at the fourth when a twenty-foot putt dropped. He had another birdie at the fifth, but the 46-year-old American fought back. However, he still trailed by two holes at the thirteenth and saw his hopes finally disappear in the Beardies. Huggan ended victor by 3 and 2.

Rajee Mohta, the Indian national champion, very nearly beat Duncan Evans, the defending holder, who snatched victory with a saucy putt. He left Mohta's ball

Philippe Ploujoux was the first continental ever to win the British Amateur Championship.

132

half-an-inch from the hole at the seventeenth, then cannoned a six-foot putt in-off for a match-winning four. Boxall departed after being two up with five to play against Jacques Lebreton, who won three holes in a run and the match by one hole. Scotland had a depressing day. Among those who lost were Donald Jamieson, Gordon Murray, Allan Brodie and Keith MacIntosh. Peter Deeble beat Guy Coles, son of Neil, by 5 and 4. The experienced Charlie Green did the same to Lionel Platts's youngster, Christopher, by 7 and 6. Gary Player's son went down to Nigel Roland on the last green, but Joe Carr's son, John, upheld the family reputation by beating Roger Witchlew 3 and 2. Ronan Rafferty, then an overweight 17-year-old, lost to Colin McLachlan. The Scot was three up with five to play, but scraped home on the last green, a tight finish after lowering the Old Course amateur record with a six under par a few days earlier.

Shocks continued on the second day, in wretched weather. The title holder lost to Alan Foster by one hole. Paul Way, winner of the Brabazon, was beaten at the twentieth. The Spanish hope, Jesus Lopez, went down to Michael Hughesden. Torrential rain in the afternoon caused play to be postponed for three hours and after the restart twenty matches had to be shelved for a 7 am start the next day. Charlie Green, a Walker Cup selector who had retired from international golf two years before, enjoyed an Indian summer at 48 by beating the British junior international Platts by 7 and 6, Philip Walton 2 and 1, then the Italian champion, Andrea Canessa by 3 and 2.

The midway stage saw many hopes disappear. Chapman was beaten by Andrew Sherborne; the seeded Canadian champion, Douglas Roxburgh, lost to the unfancied Glamorgan golfer, Glyn Davies; McEvoy was beaten by the American, Joel Hirsch; Gordon Brand, the Portuguese champion, went down to 17-year-old David Curry. John Carr continued to impress, taking the lead against MacKenzie at the Road Hole, and halving the eighteenth; the South African, van Niekerk, lost by 4 and 2; Geoff Godwin joined him by losing at the twenty-first. Malcolm Lewis beat the French champion, Illouz; Davies lost to Deeble, who found Philippe Ploujoux too strong. Scotland's last survivor was Colin Dalgleish. The Americans, Ojala and Kelley, were beaten by the Australian, Gresham. In the quarter-finals Carr squared his match against Lewis at the Road Hole by sinking a 22-footer, and repeating the feat at the eighteenth. Ploujoux was in devastating form. He needed only single putts on five of the first six holes and beat Dalgleish 3 and 2. Dunsire lost 4 and 3 to Gresham. The all-American clash between Randolph and Hirsch ended in the latter winning 2 and 1.

Ploujoux became the first Continental to reach the Amateur Championship final when he beat Carr 2 and 1. His opponent, Hirsch, went through by the same margin. In the final Philippe Ploujoux was inspired on the greens and his short game was flawless. Four up at lunch, he ran out winner by 4 and 2. The Frenchman was a worthy champion after a week in which many reputations were bruised.

Severiano Ballesteros
1984

St Andrews had cause to remember the 1984 Open Championship because it produced a champion unlike any of the previous winners of the title on the Old Course. He was unmistakable, a flamboyant shot-maker with a cavalier style almost reminiscent of Walter Hagen with a d'Artagnan touch; in short, Severiano Ballesteros, the Spaniard from Santander. He had stamped his personality on the professional scene in Europe and America, but had not taken to St Andrews, which was not surprising for the Old Course is harsh on vicious hooks and only remarkable recovery powers avoid disaster. Watching Ballesteros in action can be a palpitating experience. Occasionally his immense talent has been affected by a temperament which quickly becomes depressed. It coloured his opinion of the American tournament circuit, not always complimentary, but it did not stop him winning the US Masters in 1980 and 1983. The 1979 Open win at Lytham was decisive and now the victory at St Andrews. Triumphs such as these more than proved his powers, though probably the success that brought greatest satisfaction was the Madrid Open which earned the acclaim of his fellow-countrymen.

One of Ballesteros's ambitions was to tame the Old Course, and in particular the Road Hole which he ranks as the finest hole in the world. He won the title but did not beat the Old Course; the seventeenth is still a jinx-hole. Over the four rounds he had three bogeys, but he was not alone. During the Championship only eleven birdies were carded and it was estimated that the full entry amassed a cumulative total of 355 over par.

Determined challenges came from Bernhard Langer who was to win the 1985 US Masters, Lanny Wadkins, Greg Norman, Fred Couples and Ian Baker-Finch, but by the last round the issue was between Ballesteros and Tom Watson. At the fourteenth the Spaniard had an invaluable birdie, while Watson took three at the thirteenth. Both players were level at eleven under par with Langer two shots behind. The Championship reached its climax at the Road Hole. Ballesteros stifled his fears and placed a bold second shot on the green, but just missed a three. Watson had a par at the sixteenth. In the three previous rounds he had taken a bogey, double-bogey and a par at the Road Hole. This time he was over-strong with a No. 2 iron and finished on the road, leaving a nasty shot near the wall on the far side of the road. He succeeded in placing the ball within eight yards of the hole, but missed the vital putt. It was his last chance. Ballesteros struck a telling pitch shot to the home green and sank the putt for a birdie and the title.

More golfing history was made at St Andrews that week. The attendance of 193,000 was a record compared with the previous one of 141,000 at Birkdale the year before and prompted a 10 per cent increase in the prize fund for the professionals. Another sign of the times was the arrival by Concorde of thirteen players from the US, including Johnny Miller, Ben Crenshaw, Fuzzy Zoeller, Ray Floyd, Arnold Palmer, Andy Bean and Bill Rogers. The trip took just over 3½ hours and Concorde landed at nearby RAF Leuchars. On the Tuesday before the Championship began, Jack Nicklaus received an Honorary Degree of Doctor of Law. It was the first time the University had conferred a degree for sport and was 'in recognition of his services to the Bobby Jones Memorial Trust' which had been set up in 1974 to establish

Severiano Ballesteros won one of the most exciting Open Championships of recent history.

exchange scholarships between the University of Emory in Atlanta, Georgia, and St Andrews. During the Laureation Address, Nicklaus was described as 'a brilliant embellishment to the game and the profession, a great ambassador for the United States'. In reply Nicklaus described the Open as 'the most cherished international golf championship on earth' and said that St Andrews was his favourite venue in the golfing world. The compliment could be reciprocated, for Jack Nicklaus is a favourite adopted son of St Andrews.

S. Ballesteros (Spain)	69–68–70–69 – 276
T. Watson (USA)	71–68–66–73 – 278
B. Langer (West Germany)	71–68–68–71 – 278
F. Couples (USA)	70–69–74–68 – 281
L. Wadkins (USA)	70–69–73–69 – 281
G. Norman (Australia)	67–74–74–67 – 282
N. Faldo (GB)	69–68–76–69 – 282

Tom Watson in trouble at the Road Hole in 1984.

CHAPTER 8
THE WALKER CUP MATCHES

THE WALKER CUP MATCHES

ON 21 MAY 1921 the first amateur international match between Great Britain and the United States of America took place on the links at Hoylake. It was a full-scale test with very strong teams. The Americans were headed by 'Chick' Evans, Bobby Jones and Francis Ouimet, while we had players like Cyril Tolley, Roger Wethered, Sir Ernest Holderness and Tommy Armour. The result favoured the visitors by 9 matches to 3.

It was not until the following year that the Walker Cup match came into existence, largely due to the enthusiasm of George Herbert Walker, then President of the USGA, during discussions with a Royal and Ancient committee. On his return to the States, the American Executive Committee agreed to donate an International Challenge Trophy open to all countries who wished to send teams. Newspapers emphasised the value of such international rivalry and christened the trophy the Walker Cup. No country was in a position to accept the invitation that year, but the Royal and Ancient announced that a team would be sent to America to compete for the Cup in 1922. By then Howard Whitney had succeeded George Walker as USGA president, but,

George Herbert Walker, President of the United States Golf Association, was the initiator of the Walker Cup match in 1922.

as a gesture, Walker's home club, the National Golf Links of America, was chosen as the venue. Located near fashionable Southampton, about 100 miles from New York, in those days before the highway system had been built, it was quite a stiff run by car.

There were the usual inaugural hiccups. Ouimet used to recall the upset when the local police, acting under the impression that the Club was private property, tried to exclude the press. Then, after raising the Stars and Stripes, the members could not find a Union Jack. Two match incidents were notable. Robert Harris, the British captain, fell ill and his place was taken by *The Times* golf correspondent, Bernard Darwin, who beat William Fownes in the singles by 3 and 1 after losing the first three holes. Sweetser lost to C. V. Hooman on the 37th. Match playoffs were discontinued after that. The match ended with an American victory by 8 matches to 4, a result not unexpected because every player in that first American team was either a past winner of the national amateur title or a prospective one.

And so to the Walker Cup matches that have been held at St Andrews.

This was the Walker Cup match the British should have won. The team was strong all the way: Tolley, Wethered, Mackenzie, Hope, Harris, Hooman, Holderness, W. A. Murray, and John Wilson. Mackenzie played only in the singles and Hooman in the foursomes. It began promisingly with Roger Wethered, fresh from winning the Amateur Championship at Deal, and Cyril Tolley beating Francis Ouimet and Jesse Sweetser by 6 and 5. Ernest Holderness and W. L. Hope beat G. V. Rotan and S. D. Herron by one hole. Willie Murray and John Wilson accounted for Howard Johnstone and J. F. Neville 4 and 3. Only Robert Harris and C. V. L. Hooman lost. Even so, 3–1 was a healthy start. The Americans needed 6 wins to retain the Cup, and that from 8 singles. Wethered looked promising at 2 up with 3 to play, but Ouimet fought back with 3–4–3 against the Englishman's 4–4–4, halved the match and equalled the course record of 70 in the process. Rotan had a seemingly hopeless task, being 6 down after 14 holes, but again the come-back was killing. The American took 11 of the next 12 holes and Mackenzie lost by 6 and 4. W. L. Hope went into lunch one up against Marston, but lost 5 and 4. Holderness was 2 up with 3 to play against Wright, who rallied to win the last three holes, sinking a long putt for a birdie at the 18th and victory. Gardner beat Harris with a scrambled four at the home hole. The issue turned on the last match between Dr Willing and Willie Murray. All square with three to play, the American clinched the match and won the Cup by winning the 34th and 35th. The American victory was due to the superb fight back by the whole team.

Robert Harris, who played in the 1923 Walker Cup match.

Right:
Cyril Tolley beat Jesse Sweetser 3 and 1 in the singles and teamed up with Roger Wethered to beat Francis Ouimet and Sweetser by 6 and 5.

Foursomes

Great Britain		USA	
R. H. Wethered & C. J. H. Tolley (6 and 5)	1	F. Ouimet & J. Sweetser	0
R. Harris & C. V. L. Hooman	0	R. Gardner & M. Marston (7 and 6)	1
E. W. E. Holderness & W. L. Hope (1 hole)	1	G. V. Rotan & S. D. Herron	0
J. Wilson & W. A. Murray (4 and 3)	1	H. R. Johnstone & J. F. Neville	0
	3		1

Singles

Great Britain		USA	
R. H. Wethered	0	F. Ouimet	0
C. J. H. Tolley (3 and 1)	1	J. Sweetser	0
W. W. Mackenzie	0	G. V. Rotan (6 and 4)	1
W. L. Hope	0	M. Marston (5 and 4)	1
R. Harris	0	R. Gardner (1 hole)	1
E. W. E. Holderness	0	F. Wright (1 hole)	1
J. Wilson (1 hole)	1	S. D. Herron	0
W. A. Murray	0	Dr Willing (2 and 1)	1
	2		5

Grand Aggregate: Great Britain 5: USA 6 (One match halved)

144

The 1926 match was another might-have-been affair. Both sides were strong. The Americans included men like George von Elm, Jesse Sweetser, who had just won the Amateur Championship at Muirfield, and the formidable Bobby Jones. Foursomes went to America by 3–1. Wethered combined well with Holderness to beat Ouimet and Guilford 4 and 3, but Harris and Hezlet were murdered 8 and 7 by Sweetser and von Elm. Tolley paired with Jamieson against Jones and Watts Gunn and lost 4 and 3. Storey and Brownlow narrowly failed by one hole against Gardner and the 17-year-old Roland MacKenzie.

The singles were close and tense. Charles Hezlet settled for a half against von Elm. Andrew Jamieson contributed a sound win against Gardner by 5 and 4. Eustace Storey collected a useful point against MacKenzie by 2 and 1. Brownlow was outclassed on the day against Watts Gunn by 9 and 8. Robert Harris defeated Jesse Guilford 3 and 1, but Ernest Holderness went down 4 and 3 to Jesse Sweetser, whilst Cyril Tolley was devastated 12 and 11 by Bobby Jones. No mercy was shown by either side, but if only Hezlet had beaten von Elm on the last green! The Cup was lost by a couple of inches.

Foursomes

Great Britain		USA	
R. H. Wethered & E. W. E. Holderness (4 and 3)	1	F. Ouimet & J. Guilford	0
R. Harris & C. O. Hezlet	0	J. Sweetser & G. von Elm (8 and 7)	1
C. J. H. Tolley & A. Jamieson, jun	0	R. T. Jones & Watts Gunn (4 and 3)	1
E. F. Storey & W. Brownlow	0	R. Gardner & R. Mackenzie (1 hole)	1
	1		3

Singles

Great Britain		USA	
C. J. H. Tolley	0	R. T. Jones (12 and 11)	1
E. W. E. Holderness	0	J. Sweetser (4 and 3)	1
R. H. Wethered (5 and 4)	1	F. Ouimet	0
C. O. Hezlet (halved)	0	G. von Elm (halved)	0
R. Harris (3 and 1)	1	J. Guilford	0
W. Brownlow	0	W. Gunn (9 and 8)	1
E. F. Storey (2 and 1)	1	R. Mackenzie	0
A. Jamieson, jun (5 and 4)	1	R. A. Gardner	0
	4		3

Grand Aggregate: Great Britain 5: USA 6. One match halved

The result was depressing. The eighth successive defeat. The best the British could muster was victory in one singles and one foursomes. Satisfaction, if any, went to the Scottish members of the team and their supporters in St Andrews who reacted to the 4 and 2 win by Jack McLean and Eric McRuvie over Francis Ouimet and George Dunlap as though the Cup had been won. Tony Torrance gained the singles point over M. Marston by 4 and 3. Several of the home players were outgunned and outclassed. Cyril Tolley and Roger Wethered had to tackle Johnny Goodman and Lawson Little, outstanding performers of immense power and confidence. Eric Fiddian lost to Johnny Fisher, who was in brilliant form. Leonard Crawley more than met his match in Francis Ouimet to the tune of 5 and 4. George Dunlap ousted Jack McLean 4 and 3 by the sheer exuberance of his skill. Johnny Goodman had no mercy on the veteran Michael Scott and won by 7 and 6. Sam McKinlay, a dour Scot, lost his match, but with a shade more luck in the singles might have saved his match against Moreland. Harry Bentley appeared only in the foursomes with Eric Fiddian, but crashed 6 and 5 to Moreland and Westland.

Foursomes

Great Britain		USA	
C. J. H. Tolley & R. H. Wethered	0	J. Goodman & W. L. Little (8 and 6)	1
J. McLean & E. A. McRuvie (4 and 2)	1	G. T. Dunlap & F. Ouimet	0
H. G. Bentley & E. W. Fiddian	0	G. Moreland & J. Westland (6 and 5)	1
M. Scott & S. L. McKinlay	0	M. R. Marston & H. Chandler Egan (3 and 2)	1
	1		3

Singles

Great Britain		USA	
M. Scott	0	J. Goodman (7 and 6)	1
C. J. H. Tolley	0	W. Lawson Little (7 and 5)	1
J. McLean	0	G. Dunlap (4 and 3)	1
L. G. Crawley	0	F. Ouimet (5 and 4)	1
E. W. Fiddian	0	J. Fisher (5 and 4)	1
T. A. Torrance (4 and 3)	1	M. Marston	0
E. McRuvie	0	J. Westland	0
S. McKinlay	0	G. Moreland (3 and 1)	1
	1		6

Grand Aggregate: Great Britain 2: USA 9. One match halved

Jack McLean had a follow-through with hands exceptionally high.

Opposite:
Leonard Crawley lost to Francis Ouimet by 5 and 4 in 1934.

Another disaster would raise the question of the advisability of persisting with such a one-sided contest, but, in spite of our lamentable record, the Americans were not taking chances. A young but immensely strong team headed by Francis Ouimet, sailed on the SS Bremen of the North German Lloyd line, bound for the Amateur Championship at Troon as a curtain-raiser to the Walker Cup match. Today most of these American names are forgotten. Apart from Ouimet, already a golfing legend, Johnny Goodman was their oustanding player. This chunky little man from Omaha was the natural successor to Bobby Jones, who had retired after the Grand Slam. Goodman had already achieved the rare feat for an amateur of winning the American Open Championship. At Portland in 1937 I watched him complete the double by beating Ray Billows for the American Amateur title, a finely balanced match with Goodman winning on the last green. He promised to be a threat at St Andrews. He was conscious of his record and made sure his opponents knew it.

Then there was Johnny Fisher of Cincinnati, long-legged, reticent, with crew-cut hair, a long slashing hitter with a very fast swing. He used to bend over as he addressed the ball. His long arms came through low and close to the body. He strode along on stilt-like legs at a fair pace and wasted no time fiddling about; in every way a magnificent golfer. Many of the others were equally impressive, including Bud Ward, who became American Amateur champion the next year; Charlie Yates, the happy-go-lucky protégé of Bobby Jones at Atlanta, and Charles Kocsis, with the rhythmic swing and style. I can see these players as though it were yesterday. Somehow in those days golfers were characters in their own right. It was in so many ways a different world. It is tempting to recall the 1938 Walker Cup match and compare it with those of recent years. But this is not possible. Everything was so different. It is interesting to recall what life was like in this country at that time. Today we have become blasé with Concorde shrinking space, television taking the world into the home, and taxation with inflation affecting every walk of life. In 1938 we had income tax raised by the April Budget to 5s.6d. The bank rate was two per cent, the pound was worth $4.80. Top grade petrol was raised by 1d to 9d per gallon. Instead of James Bond we had Bulldog Drummond. The first-class fare to America on the Queen Mary was £64. The British Navy was the largest in the world, outweighing the US Navy by nearly 300,000 tons, and the Russian Fleet was one-sixth the size of the Royal Navy.

In matters sporting, our Test cricketers make their current counterparts look like selling-platers. Len Hutton scored 364 runs of the England total of 903 for 7 declared. Verity finished the season with 155 wickets for an average of 15.58. Donald Budge won the Wimbledon singles title for the second year, and Helen Wills Moody beat Helen Jacobs 6–4, 6–0 to take the ladies' title for the eighth time. Max Schmeling was thrashed in one round by Joe Louis in New York. Bob Sweeney was the defending champion at Troon, Henry Cotton held the Open title. Jessie Anderson was the ladies' champion. Ralph Guldahl was the US Open champion with Densmore Shute the American PGA title-holder. If we wanted to escape from reality we could be entertained by Debroy Somers, Duke Ellington, Glenn Miller and Benny Goodman. In so many ways life was easier in those days and we did not realise it, but in golfing matters we had a headache with the Walker Cup.

To wipe out the memory of nine successive defeats, a clean sweep had been made of the old Selection Committee. The new men were Cyril Tolley, John Morrison, Thirsk, W. B. Torrance and Dickson. They worked hard and eventually chose a cross-section of talent, with John Beck as captain. Again the names mean little to the present generation. There was bespectacled Cecil Ewing, a giant of a man who wielded a 17 oz driver as

Alex Kyle played a significant role in Britain's first victory in the Walker Cup in 1938.

148

though it were a toy club. His irons were even heavier. Using a three-quarter swing, and standing with feet close together, he slashed the ball immense distances, the force almost rivalling his rigid political principles. Hector Thomson, of a quiet, retiring disposition, had won the Amateur title two years earlier by beating the Australian Jim Ferrier by two holes at St Andrews. The rest were a rare mixture of temperaments and backgrounds. Harry Bentley displayed a Northern wit funnier than he realised, a trait he still retains. Gordon Peters and Alex Kyle reflected the dour humour of Glasgow. Leonard Crawley caricatured himself, which was by no means easy. Frank Pennink was cool and reserved. Charles Stowe was a natural, uninhibited Midlander. James Bruen was oblivious of his skill and power.

On paper they looked a workmanlike side, nothing brilliant, but sound and dour, though lacking the charisma of their opponents. Then overnight the mood changed. All of a sudden there was a sparkling spirit of confidence. The trial matches did the trick. Not only did players from varying backgrounds get to know each other, but the transformation was largely due to the supervision of Henry Cotton, then at the peak of his career. Even his presence was reassuring. Here was no theoretical instructor, no pseudo-golfing doctor who could only talk and not perform, but one of the finest professionals this country has produced, who had a knack of instilling confidence in those he played with. In the trial matches he played with every member of the team in turn. Most important were his games with James Bruen.

The 19-year-old Irish youngster hit the headlines. Exceptionally strong, with powerful shoulders, he

Jimmy Bruen's method of hitting a golf ball was unique. Few could match his style with its famous 'loop' at the top of the back-swing. It ignored logic but worked for him.

played off +6 against the Standard Scratch Score, with golf breathtaking in its force and accuracy. His style was unorthodox, with a loop at the top which somehow righted itself in the downswing for the club came

149

squarely to the back of the ball. The shots were high-carrying with a flight from the right. Wrist action was flawless. At impact the ball was given a tremendous blow. The results spoke for themselves. In those days it was unusual for 70 to be broken on the Old Course. Bruen played eight consecutive rounds, all ranging from 69 to 66, any four of which would have won any Open Championship played at St Andrews. The effect on the rest of the team was remarkable. It meant an immediate raising of standards; 70 was made the norm. That was the mood when the day arrived.

Hector Thomson and Gordon Peters walking off the last green after beating Reynolds Smith and Fred Haas.

Harry Bentley's swing had the hallmark of rhythmic timing, with hands high and right side well through.

Incidents stand out. Bruen was not in an all-conquering mood, but he had already played his part, though in Bentley he had an excellent partner. They seemed to have the measure of Fisher and Kocsis, but in the end settled for a half. Peters and Thomson had the edge on Goodman and Ward. Kyle and Stowe could not get to grips with Yates and Billows, but Crawley and Pennink made no mistake against Smith and Haas.

We ended the day with the precious lead of one point.

Beck, whose captaincy and judgment proved invaluable, made an unexpected change in the singles. Instead of dropping Kyle, he rested Bentley, in spite of his outstanding contribution in the foursomes. The gamble worked, though there were shocks and surprises galore. Pennink had his spirit broken and was thrashed to the tune of 12 and 11 by Ward, who had a morning round of 67, a halfway lead of 9 up, then resumed in the afternoon with 4, 4, 3, 3 and all was over. Yates, who had won the Amateur title at Troon, continued in the same vein against Bruen, but Thomson had the better of Goodman, Peters and Kyle were shaping well, while Crawley established a useful lead over Fisher.

Then after lunch cracks began to appear. Crawley had Fisher slinging at him no fewer than six consecutive threes from the 26th to the 32nd. The American finished the match needing two fours for a 66. Stowe was having a fierce struggle against Kocsis, survived, then had a purple patch and won by 2 and 1. Thomson, Peters and Kyle collected the points. Ewing and Billows came to the last green. The Americans tried for a three and failed, but by then it was academic. We had won the Walker Cup for the first time by three points.

After years of failure, the Cup was ours. The strength of American golf had been trounced. Nothing could take away the memory of that moment at St Andrews.

Foursomes

Great Britain		USA	
H. G. Bentley & J. Bruen (halved)	0	J. Fisher & C. Kocsis (halved)	0
G. Peters & H. Thomson (4 and 2)	1	J. Goodman & M. Ward	0
A. T. Kyle & C. Stowe (halved)	0	C. Yates & R. Billows (halved)	0
L. G. Crawley & J. J. F. Pennink (2 and 1)	1	R. Smith & F. Haas	0
	2		1

Singles

Great Britain		USA	
James Bruen	0	Charles Yates (2 and 1)	1
Hector Thomson (6 and 4)	1	Johnny Goodman	0
Leonard Crawley	0	Johnny Fisher (3 and 2)	1
Charles Stowe (2 and 1)	1	Charles Kocsis	0
Frank Pennink	0	Marven Ward (12 and 11)	1
Cecil Ewing (1 hole)	1	Ray Billows	0
Gordon Peters (9 and 8)	1	Reynolds Smith	0
Alex Kyle (5 and 4)	1	Fred Haas	0
	5		3

Grand Aggregate: Great Britain 7: USA 4. One match halved

Because of the War no Walker Cup match was played until the USGA sent a team to St Andrews in 1947. The match should have been held on American soil, but post-war conditions caused a switch in venue. From the British viewpoint, the result was disappointing. Defeat in itself was not begrudged, for the Americans were superior on the two days that counted. They had more shots in the bag. They attacked the hole in a way that negated our efforts. Their victory was deserved, the margin not deceptive. Our disappointment was due to the pre-match optimism that infected everyone in St Andrews – the team, the selectors, members of the Royal and Ancient, and the town in general. It was not pep-talk to bolster up inferior skill with mock strength. It was based on facts. The trial matches held on the Old Course had revealed the extent of our potential talent. Instead of a narrow field from which to choose a team, the selectors were embarrassed by the material at their disposal.

The net had been cast wide. The side chosen looked compact and solid. The omission of H. McInally and R. K. Bell was disappointing, but there was real hope of the 1938 victory being repeated, a view helped by the Americans themselves, who in first showing were hardly impressive. An oddly assorted bunch of styles compared unfavourably with previous American teams. Their tournament experience, however, had not been gained against weak opposition. We feared that their best form might be shown only in the match proper, but not to the extent of an 8–4 beating.

Defeat was influenced by two factors. Pre-match optimism had produced an under-estimate of the opposition strength. Selecting zeal had been carried too far. Trial matches were essential, but too much was crowded into the days before the actual contest. The English Championship had been played in exhausting weather, team selection delays, further intensive practice – all had an effect on the mental and physical make-up of the team. On their showing in the Walker Cup match, and knowing what each player was capable of producing, Ewing, Kyle and Wilson played like men who were golf weary. Wilson's weariness on the last day was marked. Not all was disappointment. Those who did well were Ronnie White, Joe Carr, P. B. Lucas, Charles Stowe and Leonard Crawley.

White's round against Kammer produced the best British golf on the second day. The first five holes were halved in 3–4–4–4–5, the Birkdale player reaching the turn in 34. At lunchtime he had a lead of three holes, which in the afternoon was increased to seven up. Kammer struck back and won the ninth, tenth, twelfth and thirteenth, but White rallied to win by 4 and 3. In the foursomes White teamed with Stowe. The pairing was effective against Chapman and Stranahan. The Americans were one up at the sixth, then collapsed, and the Englishmen went into lunch six up. The Americans applied pressure in the afternoon; fourteen holes in one under fours was useful. Out in 35 then 4–3–4–4–6–4, but it was not good enough. They were beaten 4 and 3.

Stowe's putting was a feature of this match. He was one of the few outstanding natural golfers in England. Like McInally his method was devoid of frills. There was nothing graceful about the swing. He belted the ball down the fairway with a scythe-like sweep like a dour match-player. His singles clash with Stranahan was colourful. Well matched on the tees and approach shots, the American was better on the greens. Stowe was two up at the eighteenth. Stranahan squared at the twenty-first, then played the next five holes in 2–3–3–3–3 to be dormie four up. Stowe pulled back two holes, but missed the decisive putt at the Road Hole.

Joe Carr was too strong for Stanley Bishop, the American champion, winning his singles match by 5 and 3.

Stanley Bishop had a rough time and lost both his matches.

Crawley and Lucas combined well against Ward and Quick after a bad start in which Lucas fluffed his second into the burn, while the second hole was lost with three putts. That was put behind them. Brilliant golf saw a lunchtime lead of five holes, and they eventually won by 5 and 4. Lucas met his match in Chapman in the singles. Crawley's aggressive golf saw a first round lead of three up, but in the afternoon, after Ward won the first two holes, the American replied with a sequence of 3–5–3–3–3–3–3 from the sixth to the twelfth and the Englishman lost by 5 and 3. Joe Carr was guilty of under-clubbing in the foursomes. Riegel holed a 100-yard pitch for two at the ninth. The Americans went on to win by 3 and 2. The Irishman made amends by beating Stanley Bishop, the American champion, by 5 and 3. Kyle played as though he had become stale in the foursomes. Gerald Micklem was out-generalled by Riegel. Wilson looked jaded. Turnesa showed all the signs of his golfing family tradition. Stranahan was as tireless as ever. Chapman, like Bishop and Turnesa, was brilliant in patches. The non-playing captains, John Beck and Francis Ouimet, were indefatigable with their encouragement. On the days that counted the verdict went to America.

154

Foursomes

Great Britain		USA	
J. B. Carr & C. Ewing	0	S. E. Bishop & R. H. Riegel (3 and 2)	1
L. G. Crawley & P. B. Lucas (5 and 4)	1	M. H. Ward & S. L. Quick	0
A. T. Kyle & J. C. Wilson	0	F. Kammer & W. P. Turnesa (5 and 4)	1
R. J. White & C. Stowe (4 and 3)	1	R. D. Chapman & F. R. Stranahan	0
	2		2

Singles

Great Britain		USA	
L. G. Crawley	0	M. H. Ward (5 and 3)	1
J. B. Carr (5 and 3)	1	S. E. Bishop	0
G. H. Micklem	0	R. H. Riegel (6 and 5)	1
C. Ewing	0	W. P. Turnesa (6 and 5)	1
P. B. Lucas	0	R. D. Chapman (4 and 3)	1
C. Stowe	0	F. R. Stranahan (2 and 1)	1
R. J. White (4 and 3)	1	F. Kammer	0
J. C. Wilson	0	S. L. Quick (8 and 6)	1
	2		6

Grand Aggregate: Great Britain 4: USA 8

Opposite: John Beck was an indefatigable non-playing captain.

Once again the Americans demonstrated their superiority. The British played well enough, but when the chips were down their shot-making did not match up to the knife accuracy of their opponents, particularly Harvie Ward, who broke Ronnie White's undefeated record in three Walker Cup matches. There was no mistake about the 6 and 5 defeat or by the quality of golf that later earned the American Amateur Championship title in 1955 and 1956, David Blair edged out Joe Conrad by one hole. The stocky little American found a winning streak good enough to win the Amateur Championship at Lytham, the eighth time a visiting Walker Cup player had won the title. Billy Joe Patton, of the slashing style, had the measure of Philip Scrutton, whilst Don Cherry surprisingly beat Joe Carr 5 and 4. A youthful Ian Caldwell collected an invaluable point by beating Dan Morey by one hole. As regards the foursomes the least said the better, for the British ended the day with an embarrassing whitewash. Carr and White were the nearest to scraping a point, but went down by one hole to Ward and Cherry. The margin of 10–2 speaks for itself.

Foursomes

Great Britain		USA	
J. B. Carr & R. J. White	0	J. H. Ward & D. Cherry (1 hole)	1
G. H. Micklem & J. L. Morgan	0	W. J. Patton & R. L. Yost (2 and 1)	1
I. Caldwell & E. B. Millward	0	J. W. Conrad & D. Morey (3 and 2)	1
D. A. Blair & J. R. Cater	0	B. H. Cudd & J. G. Jackson (5 and 4)	1
	0		4

Singles

Great Britain		USA	
R. J. White	0	J. H. Ward (6 and 5)	1
P. F. Scrutton	0	W. J. Patton (2 and 1)	1
I. Caldwell (1 hole)	1	D. Morey	0
J. B. Carr	0	D. Cherry (5 and 4)	1
D. A. Blair (1 hole)	1	J. W. Conrad	0
E. B. Millward	0	B. H. Cudd (2 holes)	1
C. Ewing	0	J. G. Jackson (6 and 4)	1
J. L. Morgan	0	R. L. Yost (8 and 7)	1
	2		6

Grand Aggregate: Great Britain 2: USA 10

Ronnie White was one of our greatest amateurs. He possessed the mental and physical qualities of Gary Player.

Gerald Micklem had a disappointing match in 1955, failing to score a point.

The first match played between the amateurs of Great Britain and America was played at Hoylake in 1921. Fifty years later they met at St Andrews for the 23rd Walker Cup match, with Britain clinging to the memory of a solitary victory on the Old Course in 1938. There had been a drawn match at Baltimore in 1965 when the British, leading 10–5 with eight singles to be decided, had to be content with a tie not the Cup. America, as holders, retained it. In 1971 a winning streak appeared on the Old Course. Michael Bonallack captained a side that won the elusive Cup for the second time, after a see-saw struggle which could so easily have gone either way. The home side kept its nerve in the second day singles. Resolute aggression tipped the scales, but it was even closer than the 13–11 margin suggests. The result was heartwarming, and yet, somehow, it lacked the magical moments of that day in 1938.

First Day – Foursomes

Great Britain		USA	
M. F. Bonallack & W. Humphreys (1 hole)	1	J. L. Wadkins & J. B. Simons	0
C. W. Green & R. Carr (1 hole)	1	S. N. Melnyk & M. Giles	0
D. M. Marsh & G. Macgregor (2 and 1)	1	A. L. Miller & J. Farquhar	0
J. S. Macdonald & R. Foster (2 and 1)	1	W. C. Campbell & T. Kite	0
	4		0

Singles

Great Britain		USA	
C. W. Green	0	J. L. Wadkins (1 hole)	1
M. F. Bonallack	0	M. Giles (1 hole)	1
G. C. Marks	0	A. L. Miller (1 hole)	1
J. S. Macdonald	0	S. N. Melnyk (3 and 2)	1
R. Carr (halved)	½	W. Hyndman (halved)	½
W. Humphreys	0	J. R. Gabrielsen (1 hole)	1
H. B. Stuart (3 and 2)	1	J. Farquhar	0
R. Foster	0	T. Kite (3 and 2)	1
	1½		6½

First Day's Aggregate: Great Britain 5½: USA 6½

Left:
Michael Bonallack captained the 1971 winning team.

Right:
Roddy Carr being congratulated by his father, Joe, a Walker Cup veteran himself, after halving his match against W. Hyndman.

159

160

Second Day – Foursomes

Great Britain		USA	
G. C. Marks & C. W. Green	0	S. N. Melnyk & M. Giles (1 hole)	1
H. B. Stuart & R. Carr (1 hole)	1	J. L. Wadkins & J. R. Gabrielsen	0
D. M. Marsh & M. F. Bonallack	0	A. L. Miller & J. Farquhar (5 and 4)	1
J. S. Macdonald & R. Foster (halved)	½	W. C. Campbell & T. Kite (halved)	½
	1½		2½

Singles

Great Britain		USA	
M. F. Bonallack	0	J. L. Wadkins (3 and 1)	1
H. B. Stuart (2 and 1)	1	M. Giles	0
W. Humphreys (2 and 1)	1	S. N. Melnyk	0
C. W. Green (1 hole)	1	A. L. Miller	0
R. Carr (2 holes)	1	J. Simons	0
G. Macgregor (1 hole)	1	J. R. Gabrielsen	0
D. M. Marsh (1 hole)	1	W. Hyndman	0
G. C. Marks	0	T. Kite (3 and 2)	1
	6		2

Second Day's Aggregate: Great Britain 7½: USA 4½

Grand Match Aggregate: Great Britain 13: USA 11

Left:
A moment to savour — the victorious British team.
Back row: W. Humphries, R. Foster, M. Bonallack, D. Marsh, C. Green, H. Stuart, R. Carr. *Front row:* G. Marks, J.S. McDonald, G. Macgregor.

CHAPTER 9
PERSONALITIES AND CHARACTERS

CHAPTER 9
PERSONALITIES AND CHARACTERS

THIS IS A portrait gallery of twenty-six people who played a role, however slight, in th history of St Andrews. The list is a personal one. In no way is it meant to be definitive. Twenty-six is a purely arbitrary number. Certain qualities were sought, chief among them being energy, craftsmanship, wit and a dash of the unpredictable. Those who possessed any of these in high degree could hardly help enlivening the times in which they lived. Many belong to the days when golf was a game for the few and there was a friendly intimacy which today's broader canvas makes impossible. There are still great characters and personalities about, but not as there once were. Possibly the prevailing passion for equality has resulted in an anonymous mould. It is only necessary to look around at any championship. Those taking part are all as like as peas in a pod and no doubt equally good, but they lack the charisma of the personalities I have recalled. All had one thing in common . . . an enthusiasm for the game and a love of St Andrews. In that sense, they are welcome people; *personae*, in fact *gratae*.

Cyril Tolley

So often in golf, outstanding players are linked together during their spell of eminence. The triumvirate of Harry Vardon, J. H. Taylor and James Braid; the pairing of John Ball and Harold Hilton; the era of Arnold Palmer, Gary Player and Jack Nicklaus; the clashes of Bobby Jones and Walter Hagen; the list could be extended, after all 'one star differeth from another star in glory.' Inevitably the names of Cyril Tolley and Roger Wethered were joined together in achievement. Of Roger I have written elsewhere, but Cyril was a law unto himself. Majestic and dominant, he annihilated distance with a swing of rhythm that was an aesthetic joy. He combined immense power with a delicate putting touch with a free wrist. There was about him a kingly supremacy.

Cyril Tolley was born in September, 1895; served in the Royal Tank Corps from 1915–1919; gained the Military Cross and was taken prisoner. He learnt his golf at Eastbourne, but first came into prominence when he went up to University College, Oxford in October, 1919. His long line of victories began in 1920, when, although out of practice, he entered for the British Amateur Championship at Muirfield and reached the final against the American, R. A. Gardner, became three up with

Cyril Tolley was a majestic golfer of immense power and a former captain of the Royal and Ancient Golf Club.

four to play, eventually winning at the 37th with a dramatic two. From that moment he became a recognised international figure with a natural genius for the game. His successes included a further British Amateur title, but his finest victories were perhaps the French Open Championships of 1924 and 1928.

His preference was 1924 when the field was exceptionally strong and included Walter Hagen and Gene Sarazen. For the first two rounds Tolley was paired with Arnaud Massey, who had tied with Vardon in the 1911 Open. The amateur made good progress, but in the fourth round Hagen showed the strength of the opposition by returning a 66. Tolley still had six holes to play. The first four were carded in par figures, that left two fives needed to win. At the seventeenth (450 yards) he

was short, but the run-up produced a four, which meant a six was needed at the eighteenth. A slice would have been out-of-bounds, a hook behind an orchard. He played safe with an iron from the tee finishing 80 yards short in two. The pitch-and-run finished a foot from the pin. Four on the card and Hagen had been beaten by three strokes. Tolley always felt that was his best performance. The winning aggregate was 290. Four years later on the same course he took the title again with 283, aided by some prodigious putts.

Memories of St Andrews were many. The Spring Medal with a 72; the Glennie Medal with 146; the Jubilee Vase after conceding some 60 strokes to various opponents, including nineteen shots to a professor who had two strokes at the eighth, the shortest hole on the Old Course. In that competition he twice drove the eighteenth green on the same day. At St Andrews in 1924, Denis Kyle beat him in the last sixteen of the British Amateur Championship. Up to that point Tolley had been sixteen under fours for the various rounds, but Kyle, who won 3 and 2, needed only fours at the seventeenth and eighteenth for a 66. The longest match of his career, 4 hours 25 minutes, was against Bobby Jones in 1930, which the American won at the nineteenth by a stymie, before 12,000 spectators. Then in the 1936 Amateur he was up against Alex Hill who for nine holes took only 28 shots from the seventh tee to the fifteenth green.

Cyril Tolley was Captain of the Oxford and Cambridge Golfing Society from 1946–48 and Captain of the Royal and Ancient Golf Club in 1948, a term of office noted for the immense tact and skill with which he carried out his duties. It would be true to say that he and Roger Wethered were the greatest golfers ever to come from one University.

Andrew Kirkaldy

Andrew Kirkaldy was better known to an older generation as Andra, the natural successor to Old Tom Morris. he was known for his native pawkiness, the Fife accent which English ears found somewhat difficult, and a shrewd wit. He was a link between the old and the new school of professionals. I recall his comment when our Walker Cup team had a severe drubbing, 'There's nae muckle wrang with the team. They are a' fit tae win if they are on their game. Gowfers the day are saw muckle in and out ye never can tell when they are going tae be on their game or no. The hale trouble lies in the ba'. The gutta ba' wis aye reliable and ye could easy enough pick the best gowfers, but it's no the case today, for I tell ye the ba' beats the gowfer.' Although many years have passed, I can still picture the old professional seated in state by the home green during an Open Championship at St Andrews. If there was any doubt as to where he was, he could be located by the steady stream of pertinent observations upon golf matters in general. As each couple came up, he would rise from his chair until the business of holing out was finished. He would then retire to his chair until the next couple appeared over the Swilcan Bridge. I remember him describing in his closing years what he regarded as the two greatest surprises of his life. First, when he saw 70 broken in a Championship on the Old Course; second, when a professional, who shall be nameless, walked across his line of vision resplendent in dinner jacket and studded shirt-front. The spectacle was a constant topic of disdain and amazement. He was indeed a rich personality. There was only one Andra. There will never be another.

Andrew Kirkaldy was the natural successor to Old Tom Morris and formed the link between the old and new schools of professionals.

John Whyte-Melville

Few golfers know the part played by John Whyte-Melville in the historical background to the game. Others may recall the full-length portrait painted by his friend, Sir Francis Grant, an excellent detailed canvas. Whyte-Melville, putter in hand, has just completed the first hole at the road going out. His play-club lies on the ground, a caddie tees up the ball, in the background the Swilcan Bridge, Clubhouse and the Martyrs' Monument, while the waters of the bay are ruffled by a fresh breeze. Grant captured the atmosphere of the Old Course. Others may recall the well-known painting by Charles Lees, titled *The Finish of a Big Match*. Again the scene is the Old Course and the Ginger Beer Hole, where old-time matches ended and luncheon began. Many of the figures were identified by Carnegie in verse. Among them was John Whyte-Melville.

More factual is a brief entry in the Royal and Ancient Minute Book, dated 2 October 1816: 'Which day John Whyte-Melville, Esq., of Bennochy, was admitted a member.' Virtually from that date onwards he exercised considerable influence in golfing affairs. On 3 November, 1820 we find this unusual bet linked with his name: 'Sir David Moncrieffe Bart., of Moncrieffe, backs his life against the life of John Whyte-Melville, Esq., of Strathkinness, for a new Silver Club, as a present to the St Andrews Golf Club, the price of the Club to be paid by the survivor, and the arms of the parties to be engraved on the Club, and the present bets inscribed on it. No balls to be attached to it. In testimony of which this bet is subscribed by the parties thereto.' Signatures are appended.

The fountain in the town of St Andrews, erected to the memory of John Whyte-Melville.

A group of former champions before the start of the 1984 Open. *From left to right*: Kel Nagel, Peter Thompson, Tony Jacklin, Gary Player, Henry Cotton, John Selvesen (Captain, R & A), Tom Watson, Bill Rogers, Johnny Miller, Bob Charles, Fred Daly, Lee Trevino, Arnold Palmer, Max Faulkner.

The moment of victory. Severiano
Ballesteros sinks the putt that won the 1984
Open title.

John Whyte-Melville. A portrait painted for the Royal and Ancient by Sir Francis Grant, P.R.A.

Samuel Messieux by an unknown artist, a portrait which hangs in the Royal and Ancient Clubhouse.

A minute dated 25 September 1833 describes the sequel:

'Previous to Captain Halkett Craigie resigning the chair, Captain Melville rose and stated, that on 3 November 1820, a Bet having been made by the late Sir David Moncrieffe, Bart., and himself, by which it was stipulated that the survivor should purchase and present to the Club *A NEW SILVER PUTTER*, with the arms of the parties engraved on it; Captain Melville, in the most feeling and appropriate terms, expressed his deep regret that the Club had been deprived of one of its most zealous and distinguished supporters, and although he had great pleasure in fulfilling the duty that Bet imposed upon him, he could not but regret the event which had led to it; he therefore begged to present to the Club a New Silver Putter, and to suggest that the Gold Medals should be attached to it, so that as the Silver Club handed down to posterity the names of those who had presided over its meetings, the Putter might transmit, in a similar manner, the names of those who had signalised themselves by the superiority of their play.'

Such is the history of the Silver Putter.

In 1853 an important resolution was proposed by John Grant, and seconded by Whyte-Melville, similar to that proposed in the Union: 'it is desirable that the Royal and Ancient Golf Club and the Union Club should be united; and that, with a view to this union being effected, every member henceforth admitted into the Golf Club shall thereby be held to become a member of the Union Club . . .' In the same year John Whyte-Melville was asked by the Committee to lay the foundation-stone of the Clubhouse, with masonic honours. In 1857, he was responsible for the change in the method of electing candidates for the Royal and Ancient. In those days one

black ball excluded, but Whyte-Melville moved the resolution that rejection of a candidate should be valid only if one black ball was put in the box for every eleven members at the ballot.

An interesting minute appears on 2 May 1860. 'Mr. Whyte-Melville moved the following resolution, which was seconded by Sir Thomas Moncrieffe, and agreed to unanimously: That this Club consider some acknowledgment to be due to the eminent services of the late Allan Robertson in improving the game of Golf and extending its practice throughout the kingdom, and are of opinion that for this purpose a moderate annuity should be purchased for his widow.'

In June 1863 addresses of congratulation were sent to Her Majesty the Queen, and to their Royal Highnesses the Prince and Princess of Wales, to mark the occasion of the Prince's marriage. The request that the Prince would become Patron of the Club was granted. A minute, bearing Whyte-Melville's signature, records that 'The Chairman therefore moved that His Royal Highness be elected a member of the Club by acclamation, which having been done, the Chairman nominated His Royal Highness as Captain for the ensuing year in the usual manner.' And at the September meeting, when Whyte-Melville, 'in the name and at the special request of His Royal Highness, took the Chair as Captain of the Club,' a golden ball, in place of silver, was attached to the Silver Club.

These disjointed extracts convey little of his golfing activities. Mount Melville, their family seat just outside St Andrews, was the scene of continual hospitality. With his wife, Lady Catherine, a daughter of the Duke of Leeds, and his son, George Whyte-Melville, the poet, novelist and sportsman, the evenings must have been stimulating and full of wit. The son used to say that he could go around the links as well and as often as his father if he had a glass of sherry before each tee-shot. He might have played better than his father, for John Whyte-Melville was not a brilliant golfer, but I doubt if he would have played as often, for the old man played until he was well over eighty-five years of age, three days every week, whatever the weather, and two rounds each of those days.

Unfortunately George Whyte-Melville was thrown from his horse and killed. The shock of losing his only surviving son, followed three weeks later by the death of his wife, crushed the old man's spirit. In 1870 the captaincy of the Royal and Ancient Club was offered to him the second time. He had held the post previously in 1823. The honour was accepted, but on 16 July he died. The committee recorded their deep regret at the death of the 'Father of the Club' and 'particularly of the uniform urbanity and courtesy with which he had discharged the duties of Chairman of Committee of Management for a period of over thirty years.' It was felt that members and past captains desired that no election to the office of captain should take place, but that the duties should be carried out by the retiring captain or the senior past captain in St Andrews. Thus passed a warm-hearted figure, the perfect host of the home of golf.

Freddie Tait was born in Edinburgh, the third son of an Edinburgh professor of physics, but in loyalty he was a true St Andrean. It was there that he learnt his golf during the summers, beginning at the age of five. He used an exaggerated St Andrews swing, not the usual slashing Fife version, but a smooth controlled movement, though at times, as Sandy Herd once recalled, the results could be erratic, as might be expected from a golfer with a reputation for driving the ball prodigious distances. So long as it flies straight all is well, otherwise exceptional recovery powers are necessary. This proved the case for Tait, whose trouble shots must have been similar to the mammoth efforts of Ballesteros. The Scot favoured an orthodox grip with the right hand underneath the shaft and would have no truck with the overlap. Iron shots were consistently good over the whole range, a standard common to the St Andrews school, particularly with pitch-and-run shots. For putting, Tait opted for a lofted cleek partially modified by taking a stance just in front of the ball.

Of Tait's many successes, he won virtually every important event at St Andrews. His record in the British Amateur Championship speaks for itself: in his first Amateur win he beat J. E. Laidlay, John Ball, Horace Hutchinson, and Harold Hilton in the final. Throughout his competitive career he continually came up against either Ball or Hilton. The latter he invariably beat, but Ball seemed to have the edge on him, probably because the Hoylake man was just the better player. In 1892 Tait lost in the second round; in 1893 he was beaten in the semi-final by J. E. Laidlay; in 1894 again lost in the semi-final, this time against Mure Fergusson by 4 and 3; in 1895 beaten by John Ball in the semi-final 5 and 3; in 1893 accounted for Hilton in the final 8 and 7; in 1897 beaten in the third round by W. Grieg by one hole; in 1898 won the title for the second time by beating Mure Fergusson in the final 7 and 5; in 1899 lost to John Ball in the final at the 37th. Sandy Herd used to recall several Tait occasions; one in particular was at the professional inauguration of the New Course, St Andrews when the Club held a tournament after the 1895 Open Championship. J. H. Taylor was the winner by two strokes from Herd who had led by three shots at the end of the third round. He used to say that bad luck robbed him of the title because his last round coincided with a storm and hailstones made a nonsense of putting. Herd won the New Course event with two rounds of 86, while Tait finished first amateur on 175.

Frederick Guthrie Tait should be remembered as St Andrews' and Scotland's greatest amateur. His popularity was enormous and crowds flocked to see him play. An officer in the Black Watch, he volunteered for active service in South Africa. He was only 30 when he was killed at Koodoosberg Drift and was buried by the side of the Riet River. He achieved a great deal in a short time.

Freddie Tait (right) favoured the exaggerated St Andrews swing and was Scotland's most popular amateur golfer.

Francis Ouimet

The name of Francis Ouimet was known and respected on both sides of the Atlantic for over fifty years. One end of the span went back to the Country Club at Brookline, Massachusetts in 1913 when Ouimet figured in the memorable tie for the American Open Championship with Harry Vardon and Ted Ray. The other end might be said to touch St Andrews in 1951, when he was formally installed as Captain of the Royal and Ancient.

The years between were crowded with golfing incident and achievement, but for the moment they are not our concern. I am more interested in the man than in his golfing feats. Many people eyed this bespectacled American with curiosity. He did not conform to the usual transatlantic reaction to headline success. There was no attempt to combine the wit of a jester with the skill of a genius. Ouimet appeared more at home with English conservatism than with American showmanship. His career was so different from many of his countrymen. Take Walter Hagen as an example. He started as a novelty and became an institution. Ouimet began as an unknown amateur and came to fame overnight as Open Champion. He became a senior statesman of the game. Throughout, Ouimet remained unassuming and modest to the point of self-effacement.

Ouimet was a curious mixture, a bundle of extremes. Bobby Jones recorded one of their championship matches: 'Francis was solemn as a judge; he always is in a match.' The description was justified. There was always an air of solemnity about Ouimet's play. On the other hand, it was not an aggressive mood. I recall several British golfers who tried to imitate Ouimet's mental approach to the game. All they did was to increase their blood-pressure and round-total. They became over-serious, where Ouimet was always on the verge of some light-hearted pleasantry. Few men could look back on such a successful playing career, but it was never triumph through gloom. Ouimet had his share of intense concentration, but throughout was always companionable. For that reason it was pleasing when, at fifty-eight years of age, he became the first American and the first non-British national to be honoured by election to the captaincy of the Royal and Ancient Golf Club, an office which had been held by King George VI, the Duke of Windsor and the Duke of Kent. It led to that interesting ceremony performed annually for many generations, the 'driving into office' of the new captain. The hour is early for all but enthusiasts. Golfers must need be abroad by seven-thirty in the morning if they wish to see all the preliminaries. On that occasion the morning was fair. It was late September at its best. An Indian summer with dew on the grass and waves breaking gently on the beach. Just before eight o'clock Francis Ouimet was escorted to the first tee by a group which included ex-captains Lord Balfour of Burleigh, Lord Simon, Lord Teviot, Sir George Cunningham, Bernard Darwin, Cyril Tolley and Roger Wethered. The ball was teed by Willie Auchterlonie, the club professional and Open Champion of 1893, the year Ouimet was born. The town clock struck the hour. Ouimet drove a confident ball straight down the fairway. The old-fashioned cannon, shifted from the mound behind the clubhouse, was fired with a spluttering roar. The bunched caddies rushed for the ball. The one who retrieved it from the scrimmage was rewarded with a gold American five-dollar piece instead of the former golden sovereign. The ceremony was over. Ouimet had not only played himself into office, he had won automatically the medal presented to the Club by Queen Adelaide.

It was difficult to know which aspect of his golfing career had merited the honour. As a player, Ouimet's record was impressive. Not only had he won both Open and Amateur Championships of the United States, but he played against Great Britain in the Walker Cup matches from their inauguration in 1922 until 1936, and afterwards served as non-playing captain. On the other hand, his contributions to the welfare of the game in the role of legislator and administrator were outstanding. Behind-the-scenes contributions have to be off the record. Few golfers realise the volume of administrative detail that has to be tackled by the ruling bodies. Committee work can be tedious, irritating and a waste of time, but not all comes under this heading. After World War II ended, British and American golfers played the game under different codes, which could lead to abuse and misunderstanding. I recall a conversation with Ouimet in 1947 in his hotel room at St Andrews. The Walker Cup match had just ended on an harmonious note. Ouimet emphasised that such feeling was of greater value than the actual result of international matches, but much depended on a more unified interpretation of the rules. At that time, there was a difference of opinion about the stymie.

A few years later this gulf had widened with the introduction of new British rules which reduced certain penalties and added various innovations. The danger of taking diverse paths was apparent. In May 1951, action was taken. A United States delegation travelled to this country to confer with Empire representatives. The problems were tackled with imagination. Concessions were made on both sides. Agreement was reached. The draft, with a few modifications, was approved by the USGA in July. Finally, it was ratified by St Andrews.

Francis Ouimet was a brilliant amateur and administrator. He played for America in Walker Cup matches from 1922 until 1936, and then served as non-playing captain.

The game was governed on both sides of the Atlantic by a unified code. Irregularities ended. The negotiations called for tact, patience and knowledge. In this respect, Francis Ouimet was one of the main architects in restoring Anglo-American golfing unity.

Douglas Rolland

It is interesting to compare Douglas Rolland with Edward Blackwell. The latter was renowned for prodigious individual drives, but he could not rival Rolland's consistent long hitting. Born in 1860 in Elie, Rolland worked as a stonemason from the age of thirteen and developed pronounced wrist and forearm muscles. Recorded statistics give some indication of his physique. Over six feet tall, 41½ ins chest, 12½ ins forearm, 13 stone weight, he was on a par with his even more famous cousin, James Braid, who was born in the same Fife village.

Unlike many of his contemporaries, Douglas Rolland could be casual, almost reckless, in his approach to the game. He enjoyed himself on the links and did not attempt to hide the fact. In an exhibition match against Tom Dunn at Tooting Bec, he arrived in a somewhat mellow mood, in his best clothes, hard-boiled shirt and no golf clubs. Playing with borrowed clubs, he not only trounced Dunn, but smashed the course record in the process, the only cost being a crumpled shirt. In more serious mood, Rolland got backing to accept the challenge issued from Hoylake that John Ball, rated No. 1 in the world, would play any amateur. The Scot finished nine up at Elie, eventually winning 11 and 10 at Hoylake. A repeat match the next day saw Rolland 5 down with 6 to play, but he managed to win all the remaining holes. Rolland turned professional in 1887. Although highly successful in challenge matches, he never won the Open Championship. The Old Course proved too difficult to master, the penal bunkers taking a toll of his mighty hitting.

W. T. Linskill

W. T. Linskill was a rare personality who revelled in recalling St Andrews of the past, was fascinated by ghost stories, regretted he had never seen one, was almost a custodian of the Old Course, and delighted in claiming that he introduced golf to Cambridge. He was the son of Captain Linskill, Mayor of Tyneside and the Hon. Mrs Linskill, was educated at Jesus College, Cambridge, and made first contact with St Andrews on holidays with his parents, becoming a golfing enthusiast, with Young Tom Morris as his tutor. He was elected a member of the Royal and Ancient Golf Club in 1875.

Linskill's claim to have introduced the game to Cambridge was perhaps slightly exaggerated, though unquestionably his enthusiasm led to the inauguration of the match between Oxford and Cambridge Universities. Keenness was certainly needed to justify the early start for these matches, the wearisome journey to London, the drive to Waterloo, train to Putney, another conveyance to the London Scottish Iron Hut, well-earned lunch, and eventually a round of golf to decide the issue for a year. As regards the beginning of golf in Cambridge, this is what Linskill himself had to say on the subject: 'It was in 1873 when I first started the game at Coe Fen and Sheep's Green amid much derision and chaff. I taught one or two chaps to play and finally we discovered Coldham Common and started a club there. I cut the holes, rolled the greens, marked the tees and minded clubs, also acted as teacher. No one knew this Scottish game and nearly everyone despised it.' He failed to record that this Coldham Common course had abominable lies through the green and a poisonous smell from an adjoining glue-works which at times made the playing of the far holes almost impossible. This claim was questioned by Lord Dunedin when addressing the committee of the Cambridge University Golf Club in King's College. He questioned Linskill's statement, 'It seemed to me impossible that in 1873 the only people who knew golf in Cambridge were people who were taught by Linskill. There must have been Scotch boys who had surely played golf at home, for I well remember a former generation, even a generation in front of me, who, although they did not play golf at Cambridge, had played it in Scotland. One of my predecessors was William Muir, who won, very shortly afterwards, the St Andrews Medal. I do not want to take away from Mr Linskill the great credit to which he is entitled. I think he was the founder of your club, and certainly he was the first person who brought off university matches, but I do not think he was the founder of golf at Cambridge.'

Lord Dunedin added personal reminiscences: 'I learned golf first in 1866. It was quite true that I had a golf club long before that. I was given a golf club by a tutor. He taught me to play in the beginning of June 1857. I was in Perthshire at the time and an inland links was utterly unknown. It was supposed that you could only play golf by the sea-shore or on the banks of a river, so I only began golf in Edinburgh during my holidays from Harrow at Musselburgh in 1866. When I became eighteen in 1868 I was elected a member of the Honourable Company of Edinburgh Golfers. I came up to Cambridge for my first term in October 1868. I cannot remember if I brought my clubs with me in 1868, but I certainly did in 1869 and I went out and practised by myself on Midsummer Common.

'Towards the close of the forties the parson at Northam Burrows in Devonshire, not far from Bideford, was a certain Mr Gosset. His sister married one of the Moncrieffs of St Andrews. Gosset went up there to visit his brother-in-law and his new relations taught him golf. Being a sensible man, he considered that there was a place where golf could be played near his own home and they began to play golf in a desultory sort of way at Northam Burrows, which ended finally with the Westward Ho Club being founded in 1864. Gosset had a son George, who was at King's the same time as I was. He had also thought about golf and he started playing on Midsummer Common with another King's man. It came to the knowledge of us two and we made friends upon the strength of it. We put our heads together and came to the conclusion that Midsummer Common was no use. In the first place it was a place where you really could not have a links; secondly, you could get into frightful trouble for hitting people; so, wondering where we could go, we thought we would go and prospect at Royston.'

Their method was primitive as all beginnings are in golf, be it Fife or Hertfordshire. 'Gosset and I went over to Royston one day accompanied by two bags of clubs and a hole-cutter which he had brought from Westward Ho. In Royston we picked up three little boys and went to the heath. Surveying the land, we started, and decided here should be the eighteenth hole and the tee shall be here. We settled that the first hole should be a long one and we looked with our eye and fixed the spot where the hole should be. We hit two full shots and then we played the approach shot. Then we cut the hole – and remember the hole was not cut in the way of making an isosceles triangle of which the base was the line between our two balls – it was honestly kept where we said it would be, and we did the putting. We went through the eighteen holes like that, and I really believe that is probably a unique round of golf. When we returned we spoke to our friends and inserted an advertisement in the paper.'

Claude Carnegie, a Scotsman who lived in Forfar, added a footnote. He wrote to Lord Dunedin, 'I have no record of the club but what really happened was this – that in response to an advertisement seventeen of us turned up, including Gosset, you and myself. Gosset was elected captain, I was appointed honorary secretary and I took the names and 2s.6d. from everybody. So far as I remember this was in 1869. The end of the term came soon after and the following term I could not get them together again. Some went down, some said Royston was too far off, many never answered my letters, so I was left to only five or six faithfuls.'

Lord Dunedin concluded, 'By the end of 1871 everybody went down and nothing more happened. There was some contemporary knowledge of this because there was a letter on 13 November 1869 to *The Field* stating that a club had been formed and describing a match between Gosset and another King's man against myself, playing one ball.'

This evidence would seem to suggest that W. T. Linskill was the inaugurator of the University Match, but credit for founding the first golf club and introducing the game to Cambridge should go to Lord Dunedin, though I am sure golf must have been played in and around Cambridge much earlier than 1869. It had been played in Scotland for over a century and it is unlikely that Scottish youths left their clubs at home when they crossed the Border. Cambridge University records the progress of Linskill in every University Match. In the first contest on a windswept Wimbledon Common in March 1878, he failed to win a single hole against W. S. W. Wilson of Exeter. Oxford, under the captaincy of Horace Hutchinson, who was to become Amateur Champion at St Andrews eight years later, ended the day victors by 24 holes to nil. The following year Cambridge had revenge by 12–2, but Linskill lost by one hole to Andy Stuart, in spite of sinking long putts with his wooden putter which he wielded so effectively in later years on the Old Course. In 1882, Linskill, still captain of the CUGC, failed again against Ludovic Grant of Balliol, but the Light Blues won 8–7. Finally in 1883 he ignored the Four Years' Rule, and again turned out for Cambridge. This time he halved with Grant, but Oxford gained the day by 15–13. So ended Linskill's reign as Tchekhov's eternal student in favour of a more mature role in St Andrews.

His interests as Dean of Guild were numerous. Inspired by visits to the catacombs of Rome, he was convinced that an underground passage existed between St Andrews cathedral and the castle, which to his delight seemed confirmed after a subterranean passage was discovered when a cottage near the castle was demolished in 1879. Not so successful were his delvings into the supernatural, as he tried to trace records of hauntings amid the ruins of St Andrews. Many of these stories he committed to paper. The effect tended to be somewhat flowery, hardly on a par with *Tales of the Unexpected* on television, but they never lacked imagination. For twenty-five years he contributed in more practical fashion on the St Andrews Town Council. In private he never tired of relating how he escaped death on the train that plunged from the Tay Bridge in December, 1879. He was travelling from Edinburgh to St Andrews with the usual change at Leuchars, where a cab was expected to be waiting. Delayed by the stormy conditions, Linskill decided to continue by train to Dundee. Just as it was about to leave a porter called out that the cab had

176

arrived. Linskill and a friend who was travelling with him jumped out of the train as it began to move. Both lives were saved by seconds.

Much about Linskill has a Pickwickian touch: in red coat he used to drive from King's Cross to Wimbledon Common in a four-in-hand coach complete with guard and post-horn. His recollections of the Old Course went back to the time of reclamation work on the edge of the first fairways, and were recorded in an article to *Chamber's Journal*: '. . . between the Royal and Ancient Golf Club and the burn at the first hole, many acres of land have been reclaimed from the German Ocean. Where I can remember the sea-shore once existed, there are now excellent lies for the players' balls. There are, I believe, three sea-walls buried under the golf green, and the old bathing-place was once under the present window of the north room of the Club. The historic Swilcan Burn formerly swept almost into the centre of the Links before it turned into the sea, and one often drove into this bed from the first tee. It was then a sandy natural hazard, but now it is a concrete-walled channel.'

Not all was research into architectural and supernatural mysteries. He knew how to enjoy himself. In company with Young Tom Morris and others like-minded, he used to play moonlight matches. The routine was two rounds, with dinner in-between, on the Ladies' Putting Course, with candles placed in the holes, a formal version of an impromptu match late at night before a Walker Cup Match and doubtless equally lighthearted.

W. T. Linskill died on 22 November 1929, aged 74. He left behind the memory of a portly figure, familiar high collar, high spats and drooping moustache, deceptively pugnacious, for at heart he was a gentle character with a weakness for romantic legends and a passion for golf.

Of all the eminent golfers who have played on the Old Course, not many have equalled the dramatic appeal of James Bruen. Few of the present generation saw him play and possibly have no idea who he was, but those who saw him will never forget the strangest style first-class golf has known. His swing had to be seen to be believed. He took the club back outside the line of flight, then turned his wrists inward so sharply that at the top of the backswing the clubhead pointed in the direction of the tee-box. It was then swept inside and down into the hitting zone with tremendous power. The loop at the top of swing contradicted all known theories about the arc of swing. The whipping action aided acceleration and produced abnormal length.

I first saw him play in the Boys' Championship at Birkdale in 1936. He made mincemeat of the opposition that week. In the final he thrashed young Innes by 11 and 9. His potential was obvious; the only danger was too early success. He did not get far in his first British Amateur Championship. Richard Chapman had no mercy. A turbulent second round match put the Irish lad on the sidelines. He was then seventeen years of age. The following season saw the early promise come to fruition in the Walker Cup trials at St Andrews. Bruen played nine rounds over the Old Course and only once needed more than 71. The first round was 68. The next three cards beat Bobby Jones's record aggregate of 285 in the 1927 Open Championship. The comparison was perhaps not fair because Jones had been playing under strain. Nevertheless, the quality of Bruen's golf was remarkable. It was asking too much to expect the Irishman to repeat the performance in the Walker Cup match itself. The gallery expected cards of under 70, but golf is not like that. Results are not penny-in-the-slot

177

efforts. The sparkle temporarily deserted the Irish boy.

Bruen's game became somewhat bogged down. In the 1939 British Amateur Championship he did well until he met Alex Kyle. The Scotsman's game was then at its peak. The result was never in doubt. The Open Championship at St Andrews saw Bruen bracketed alongside Henry Cotton as joint favourite. Qualifying rounds confirmed the ranking: 69 on the Old Course was matched with a similar card the next day on the New. His total of 138 led the field by four shots. But once again the zip disappeared at the critical moment. In the Championship, Bruen began with a 72 and ended with a 76 to finish first amateur and equal seventh in the list. It was a performance that would satisfy any amateur, yet it fell short of what was expected.

It is idle to speculate what might have happened had the war years not intervened. I believe we had in Bruen an amateur capable of winning the Amateur and Open titles on both sides of the Atlantic had he taken the trouble to work at his game. The British Amateur Championship of 1946 supplied the answer in part. There was an entry of 260. Form was in the melting-pot.

Pre-war reputations meant next to nothing. The record book shows that Bruen won by beating Robert Sweeny 4 and 3. It looked impressive, but I question whether our main amateur honour has ever been won with the assistance of so many recovery shots. No one claimed that Bruen had a graceful style. Purists damned it outright as ugly. He drove the ball prodigious distances, but excessive length without control can be disastrous. In Bruen's case it proved distracting without being fatal. His efforts to extricate himself from unplayable lies resulted in three smashed clubs. I remember one hole in particular in that final. Playing against a strong wind and in torrential rain, he carded a 517-yard hole in two glorious shots. Bruen deserved the Amateur title, but it was not won with golf worthy of his skill.

James Bruen was a law unto himself, endowed with the concentration of Locke, the skill of Hogan and the consistency of Jones. If only his enthusiasm had lasted a few more seasons to build on the skill that enabled a lad of nineteen to lead the field of Open professionals over the Old Course by four strokes. There will never be his like again.

'Black Care may ride behind the horseman: he never presumes to walk with the caddie.'

Lord Balfour

Samuel Messieux

Samuel Messieux, a Swiss, went to Dundee in 1815, lodged in the Overgate with his friend, the poet Thomas Hood, and took private pupils in French. Later he moved to St Andrews and accepted a teaching post in the United College, eventually switching to Madras College for a similar appointment. This gave him the opportunity to play golf and get to know the Old Course. Carnegie of Pitarrow refers to Messieux in his poem *Golfiana*, published in 1833:

> Here's Monsieur Messieux, he's a noble
> But something nervous, that's a bad affair,
> It sadly spoils his putting, when he's press'd,
> But let him win and he will beat the best.

As to that there was no doubt, for in 1825 he won the Gold Medal of the Royal and Ancient with 105 and again in 1827 with 111, also the Silver Cross in 1840. Yet it is not by such victories that Messieux is remembered. The records credit him with a remarkable drive of 361 yards with a teed feathery ball from the Hole o'Cross green to the Hell Bunker. One of his pupils, later Professor James Stuart, recorded an eye-witness version of that day in 1836. The conditions were favourable, frosty with a slight wind behind. Doubts were expressed later as to whether such a shot was possible. The sceptics overlooked the fact that a feather ball when new and in good shape could fly farther than the gutta.

Other references to Messieux occur in Bet Books. An entry dated 9 February 1823 appears in the records of the Honourable Company of Edinburgh Golfers: 'Challenge, Secretary against Mr Messieux at St Andrews Links, each stricking to stand on one foot in the month of May'. On another occasion Messieux offered to play with his putter against Glensaddle, who in turn could use any of his clubs and he would allow his opponent a third. In 1833, Messieux gave his putting-iron to Robert Oliphant, whose son presented it to the Royal and Ancient Club in 1874.

Samuel Messieux died in 1859. His likeness is preserved in the North Room of the Royal and Ancient clubhouse in a painting by an unknown artist, showing him in a red coat holding a club with a purposeful double-handed grip.

'The least thing upset him on the links. He missed short putts because of the uproar of the butterflies in the adjoining meadows.'

P. G. Wodehouse, *The Clicking of Cuthbert*

Robert Maxwell

St Andrews crowds looked upon Robert Maxwell as the natural successor to Freddie Tait. In his heyday, spectator reaction was unforgettable. Although this Edinburgh born golfer was closely linked with East Lothian golf, in particular with Muirfield, with numerous Tantallon and Honourable Company Medals to his name, the Old Course at St Andrews was larded by this dominant but genial giant who had charismatic appeal. Everything about him – height, bulk and great physical strength – attracted the galleries. He knew it and warmed to the attention. Adrenalin flowed and for eight years he dominated the Scottish international golfing scene.

It began in 1897 when he beat John Ball at the fifth extra hole in the Amateur Championship and then went on to defeat Harold Hilton – all this at the age of 21. In the 1902 Open Championship which Sandy Herd won with 307 from James Braid and Harry Vardon who were bracketed together on 308, Maxwell had the impressive aggregate of 309, returning a last round of 74, possibly due to using the new Haskell ball. Maxwell was first amateur again in the Open of 1903, the year he became Amateur Champion through beating Horace Hutchin-son in the final by 7 and 5. In the 1909 Amateur Championship final, he was one down with two to play. At the seventeenth he evened the match with a three, and a four at the last hole was good enough to beat Cecil Hutchison. After that triumph Maxwell's championship career ended, although he played in one more international match the following season. He retired to enjoy his golf for though he found the support of galleries an encouragement, he disliked the publicity that went with it.

Looking through old photographs, it is interesting to study his style. It was certainly distinctive. The clubhead followed a wide flat arc, with hands very high at the top of the swing. The left shoulder was high in the air with a rigid left arm. The backswing was short and stiff. Stance was wide, with the right shoulder well down and the right hand under the shaft while the swing was generated by a lurch. Pitch-and-run shots were executed with a niblick. Long approach shots ruled the pin. On the greens his touch was delicate. It was not everybody's style, but it won medals galore and championships for Robert Maxwell.

'Statisticians estimate that the average of crime among good golfers is lower than in any class of the community except possibly bishops. Since Willie Park won the first Championship at Prestwick in the year 1860 there has, I believe, been no instance of an Open Champion spending a day in prison.'

P. G. Wodehouse, *The Clicking of Cuthbert*

Sandy Herd

When Sandy Herd died in 1944, the game lost one of the few remaining giants of the last century. I recall the last time I played with him. It was a long course and the wind blew strongly. Few men of his age would have persevered, but although he became very weary and those inimitable waggles decreased, he refused to give in and finished the round with one of those cunning hooks for which he was famous.

Several features about his play are associated with his name. The most obvious idiosyncrasy was his waggle. It was not an indication of indecision: on the contrary, it reflected determination to strike at the psychological moment. Apart from the effect on his game, these waggles had a disconcerting effect on his opponents. Herd also favoured the old-fashioned palm grip as opposed to the more common interlock or overlap. His best known shot was the cut-up with a spoon. It was sheer delight to watch how he found the target by this method. He was an excellent iron player and a consistent putter.

Although his golfing service was spent in England at three clubs, Huddersfield, Coombe Hill and Moor Park, Herd was first and foremost a true son of St Andrews. He was born in a humble house in North Street on 24 April 1868, and he used to say that his introduction to the game came not on the links but in North Street itself. The course stretched to Bell Street, and the 'holes' were strategic lamp-posts which had to be hit by balls made from champagne corks. His companion of similar age was Laurence Auchterlonie. The childish dreams and fancies shared at the age of seven years eventually came true. Auchterlonie went out to America and won the United States Open title, and Herd gained similar success in this country. His professional career was due

Sandy Herd, born in North Street in 1868, was a great champion and worthy son of St Andrews. He is seen here practising at Hoylake for the 1936 Open Championship, watched by S. Taggart (left) and the author in younger and slimmer days.

to David Lamb. At the time Herd was working as a plasterer for Andrew Scott, from whose yard have come three Open Champions, when he received a message asking him to go down to the links. David Lamb told him that his brother-in-law had asked if he could find a professional for the summer months at Portrush. Herd accepted and started work in 1890.

It was the beginning of a brilliant golfing career. He won the Open Championship at Hoylake in 1902 and was runner-up on four occasions. The record must be assessed against the fact that from 1900 to 1910 he was playing against the best ball of Vardon, Taylor and Braid. The Open which he won marked the arrival of the rubber-cored ball. A month before, the Amateur Championship had been played over the same links. During it the possibilities of the Haskell ball had been demonstrated when Charles Hutchings clinched a narrow win over Sidney Fry in a storm of wind and rain. The professionals would not use the new ball and preferred the gutta-percha. Herd felt the same until he had a practice round with John Ball. The Hoylake amateur, using a Haskell, beat the professional by such a margin that Herd changed his mind and switched to the new balls for the Open. The ploy worked. Vardon finished one shot behind Herd, who almost lost through over-anxiety over the closing holes. This touch of panic under pressure prevented him from repeating the Open victory. Eventually he was able to control his nerves, but by then the early enthusiasm had waned. Nevertheless, he was second to George Duncan in the 1920 Championship at the age of fifty-two, a seven at the sixteenth costing the title. Six years later he won the *News of the World* Tournament, the equivalent of the PGA Match-play Championship, after a terrific struggle in frightful weather on the 38th green. In one sense 1895 was one of his best years. He won practically everything there was to win in the professional world – except the Open. In this his chances were washed away by a cloudburst in the final round. J. H. Taylor was more fortunate. The weather cleared and the title was his.

Sandy Herd was a great golfer and a warm-hearted character. He was a true and worthy son of St Andrews.

'The player may experiment about his swing, his grip, his stance. It is only when he begins asking his caddie's advice that he is getting on dangerous ground.'

Sir W. G. Simpson, *The Art of Golf*, 1892

Edward Lyttelton

To the general public the name of Edward Lyttelton, former headmaster of Eton, was always associated with sporting activities. Three instances support this. A month or so before he died the following episode took place: 'He used always to say his evening prayers standing before the fire, with his back to it and leaning on a stick. If his walking-stick were elsewhere, he would go off and fetch it rather than do without it. I left him immersed in his prayers. When I came back he was batting away merrily in the air with his stick. After a minute or two he was again plunged in his devotions. When asked afterwards, "Were you batting?" "That may be!" was his reply, with a whimsical smile.' That story was told to me by Dr Cyril Alington, then Dean of Durham. In a similar strain was the apocryphal Lyttelton anecdote that once when he was saying his prayers in the tower room at Eton at an unconscionably early hour, he rose to his feet and picked off the Vice-provost's cat, an old enemy, with an air gun. Then there was the young man who, being interviewed on the cricket ground at Haileybury for a possible appointment, recorded his introduction to Lyttelton as follows, 'I remember being much struck by the easy and natural way he passed instantaneously from the subject of the Holy Spirit's work in the young to the excellence of a sudden brilliant stroke by one of the batsmen. It was something quite new in my experience of schoolmasters, and gave me my first impression of the soul of E.L.; his heart was in both worlds.'

I doubt whether I could with exactitude say that Edward Lyttelton was a golfer. He was interested in the game in the same way that he was interested in most outdoor pursuits. He would talk about golf, but admitted that his knowledge of the game was slight. He began to play at an age which was somewhat advanced. He played at golf but never reached that modest standard when some of the suffering which is the lot of every novice is alleviated by an occasional accurate shot. To progress beyond this stage, if the game is started when blood flows thinly and joints are not so supple, calls for considerable concentration. And as Dr Lyttelton indulged in the engrossing mental habit of composing Latin verse between shots, it was not surprising that his game did not improve. Fate obviously decided that he should never be a true golfer. The loss by theft of his first set of clubs when he was staying in St Andrews failed to act as a deterrent, but when a second set went the same way he saw the finger of Providence in the matter and with an equanimity indistinguishable from relief, abandoned the links for the garden.

One pleasure never decreased. His interest in St Andrews, its history and the background to the golfing scene. Clearly the early happenings of the ecclesiastical capital of Scotland were important. He used to talk about Bishop Reid, who seized every opportunity of playing on the Old Course and would recall innumerable stories about his distinguished golfing relative, Freddie Tait. Lyttelton was also a friend of another bishop of the Episcopal Church of Scotland and outstanding liturgical scholar, who could claim that J. H. Taylor was once his warden. Lyttelton used to comment that though, on the whole, clerics make indifferent golfers, at least those who regard St Andrews as the home of golf must be grateful to the ruthless John Hamilton, who was the last archbishop of the Roman Church. This prelate who proposed that Mary, Queen of Scots, be put to death and was himself hanged for involvement in the murder of Darnley, her husband, was the architect of the Charter drafted in 1552 which confirmed the rights of the community to the ground now occupied by the Old Course and to play golf over it. This document reserves to the Provost and Town Council and townspeople the right to use the Links for 'golfe, futeball, shuting and all games, as well as casting divots, gathering turfs and for the pasturing of their live-stock.'

The St Andrews Town Council have always been conscious of these rights. The annual custom of riding the marches or boundaries confirmed the rights of housewives to bleach washing on the Old Course as well as playing golf. There were protests that men were playing golf instead of being at church services. The Kirk Session of St Andrews Town Church rebuked their congregation in 1598 for being guilty of such offences, and Patrick Learmont, son of the St Andrews Provost, took the law into his own hand by shooting an arrow at Archbishop Adamson because he was playing on the Old Course instead of being in church. In such people

golf can induce a deteriorating effect. Not so with Edward Lyttelton. He recalled how once, late in life, he tried to convince a sceptical companion that he was no longer interested in cricket. As the short-lived argument proceeded, he flashed out, 'Well, it's certainly a rum thing, but I never go into a church without visualising the spin of the ball up the nave.'

But however we try to recall Edward Lyttelton, on the Old Course wielding a hesitant club, on the cricket pitch flashing a polished bat, or as a dignified cleric whose range of sympathy embraced the realm of sport, he remained, in the words of Dr John Murray, the personification of 'fineness and force, strength with gentleness, strictness with humour – a whole range of contrasted things, and above all, youth in age. He was really of all ages.' Certainly for me, Edward Lyttelton will always remain the perfect example of a clerical man of sport.

'I have had some curious experiences in golf in my time. For example, it is, I suggest, a coincidence that all the five holes which I have done in one stroke have ceased to exist. One ribald fellow has held that each of these five holes was doomed so soon as my ball found its way into the tine from the tee; no self-respecting green committee could, he said, endure the implied reproach. Two whole courses, Hincksey and Radley, each in turn the home of the Oxford University Golf Club, have been abolished in order to remove three of these discredited short holes. The other two were the fifteenth and sixteenth at Westward Ho! as we played it twenty-five years ago.'

A. C. M. Croome

Admiral Maitland Dougall

Admiral Maitland Dougall is remembered in St Andrews for an incident which occurred during the Autumn Meeting of 1860. Conditions were frightful. Gale force winds and torrential rain played havoc with scores. One player tackled every shot with a driving-putter, while others found the wind carrying the ball back over their heads. Reports came of a vessel in distress in the bay. The lifeboat was prepared to launch at the mouth of the Swilcan, about 200 yards from the first tee, but there was difficulty in manning it. Volunteers were reluctant to come forward. Maitland Dougall, who was about to play in the Medal, offered to help and took the stroke oar. For five hours the lifeboat was in the gale. The crew was eventually rescued, but the fishing vessel smashed on the rocks. Changing into dry clothes, Maitland Dougall completed his round on the Old Course in 112 strokes, which was good enough to win the Gold Medal.

Roger Wethered

Roger Wethered was a thoughtful golfer who played with machine-like precision. If there was a weakness, his driver was the rogue club. J. H. Taylor used to say that had Wethered used irons off the tee, the history of the Walker Cup might have been different. The veteran professional's regard for Wethered was considerable. He rated him as one of the finest amateur iron players of his day with shots of knife-like crispness, but deplored his tendency to use an iron technique with woods. The trait is common. Many golfers unconsciously model their style around their favourite shot, a habit that can be costly unless, like Wethered, recovery powers are good.

J.H. was a shrewd judge of golfing skills, but his comments on Wethered's Walker Cup record were somewhat at variance with facts. His opponents in five Walker Cup matches were Francis Ouimet, Jesse Sweetser, W. C. Fownes, Jesse Guilford, 'Chick' Evans, Robert Gardner, George von Elm, Johnny Goodman, George Voigt, Bobby Jones and Lawson Little. Against this formidable galaxy of talent, Wethered had four foursomes victories from five matches, plus a half and a win over Ouimet in the singles. The halved match against Ouimet at St Andrews in 1923 was an epic struggle, as the American recalled, 'At one hole Roger's shot was at least 40 feet from the cup on a green as fast as lightning. If he could place his putt dead, it seemed he would be accomplishing a miracle. My second left me a ten-footer. Roger putted his trans-continental putt and holed it. The shock was too much for me.' Wethered's putting touch was a determining factor in the 1923 Amateur Championship final when he beat Robert Harris by 7 and 6, but the magic deserted him in the 1930 Walker Cup match when Bobby Jones crushed him 9 and 8. Four years later, Johnny Goodman and Lawson Little beat the Tolley-Wethered pairing by 8 and 6. The 1921 Open Championship at St Andrews figures prominently in the golfing record of Roger Wethered, but is dealt with in the section on Jock Hutchison.

Roger Wethered's term of office as Captain of the Royal and Ancient Golf Club in 1946 added fresh dignity to the illustrious roll.

Roger Wethered, a thoughtful golfer who played with machine-like precision.

S. Mure-Fergusson

In the summer of 1898, Coburn Haskell of Cleveland completed his experiment with a rubber-filled golf ball, an innovation which caused an upheaval among the legislators. Among those opposed to the idea when the subject was discussed by the Rules of Golf Committee in September 1902 was S. Mure-Fergusson who moved that 'the new rubber-filled balls are calculated to spoil the game of golf as now played over Links laid out for the gutta ball, and that it would be advisable to bring in a new rule for the regulation of balls and clubs to be used in playing the game.'

The diehard opposition failed, but it was several years before this intimidating St Andrews golfer would acknowledge the change that revolutionised the game. As a golfer, Mure-Fergusson ranked as one of the finest amateurs never to win the Amateur Championship, though he did reach the 1894 final only to be beaten by John Ball at the last hole. As a stylist, he was a one-off. Action photographs and contemporary comments suggest a swing not noted for elegance. Although he learnt his golf at St Andrews, he did not inherit its full classic flowing style. He took the club back so that at the top of the swing the hands were unusually high, then lunged forward into a sweeping finish. His favourite stroke, particularly effective in the wind, was a glorified push-shot with a driving mashie in which the club was taken back a very short distance with wrists kept rigid, the ball being virtually pushed with an arm action. This stiff-armed shot was a stroke-saver in gusty conditions. Immensely powerful, Mure-Fergusson was frequently wild off the tee, but compensated on the greens, using a lofted cleek. All his shots appear to have been played with very much the same grip and stance.

William St Clair of Roslin

The St Clair line was founded at the time of the Conqueror. William de Sancto Claro was an Anglo-Norman baron who settled in Scotland during the reign of David I, who conferred on him the barony of Roslin, confirmed to his son, Sir William, in 1180. His descendants acquired the Earldom of Orkney and from their offspring the Earldom of Caithness. The William St Clair of our concern, who was Captain of the Royal and Ancient Golf club in 1764 and 1768, was born in 1700 and married Cordelia, daughter of Sir George Wishart of Clifton Hall. All his family died young and he was the last of the line.

His life is well-documented. He was the last to occupy the office of the Hereditary Grand Master of the Freemasons of Scotland, but voluntarily resigned and became the first elected Grand Master. As a man he was very tall and powerfully built. Sir Walter Scott records his impressions, in *Provincial Antiquities* with the pen-portrait, 'a man considerably above six feet, with dark-grey locks, a form upright, but gracefully so, thin-flanked and broad-shouldered, built, it would seem, for the business of the war or the chase: a noble eye of chastened pride and undoubtedly authority, and features handsome and striking in their general effect, though somewhat harsh and exaggerated when considered in detail. His complexion was dark and grizzled, and, as we schoolboys who crowded to see him perform feats of strength and skill in the old Scottish games of golf and archery used to think and say amongst ourselves, the whole figure resembled the famous founder of the Douglas race . . . in all the manly sports which require strength and dexterity, Roslin was unrivalled, but his peculiar delight was archery.'

Scott also recorded that each man admitted to the Royal Company of Archers was reminded by Roslin that his duties were to act as the King's Bodyguard whenever the King came to Edinburgh. As a golfer, St Clair's successes came in middle life. His signature first occurs in a Royal and Ancient minute of 1763. The following year he won the Silver Club in 121 strokes over 22 holes. He was the only stroke winner of the Silver Club over this distance. The next day, 4 October 1764, as new Captain, he signed a minute which stated that 'The Captain and Gentlemen golfers present are of opinion that it would be for the improvement of the Links that the first four holes should be converted into two. They therefore have agreed that for the future they shall be played as two holes, in the same way as presently marked out.' It would seem that one hole was removed from between the eighteenth and the Burn Hole; the other from between the Burn Hole and the corner of the Dyke, making eighteen, as the same holes were played both ways.

St Clair's score of 121 works out as 99 for the eighteen holes, which for a man of 64 was good going. In 1761 and again in 1771 he was Captain of the Honourable Company of Edinburgh Golfers. At the Spring Meeting of 1776, he won the Silver Club given by the town of Edinburgh, and in the same year he returned a score of 103 at St Andrews. A couple of years later, at the age of 68, he won again with 106. It was his last golfing success, though he competed for two more seasons. He died in 1778 and Scott described how when he was buried in the Roslin Chapel, the bases of the pillars 'were slightly indented to make room for his corpse, in consequence of his uncommon stature.'

His likeness is preserved in a painting completed in 1771 by Sir George Chalmers, commissioned by the

Honourable Company of Edinburgh Golfers. Robert Clark recorded 'this fine picture was disposed of at the Sale of the Club's effects in 1831. It is now in the hall of the Royal Company of Archers – a copy hangs in the Clubhouse of the Honourable Company.' The artist painted his subject full-length in golfing dress with meticulous attention to detail. From a golfing point of view, the stance is interesting. The left foot is well in front and the right set so well back that the left foot is midway between it and the ball. The position looks uncomfortable, but the length of the early clubs made such a position necessary if the club was to swing fluently. Certainly William St Clair had mastered that technique.

Silver statuette of William St Clair of Roslin, Captain of the Royal and Ancient Golf Club in 1764 and 1768. His signature first occurs in a minute of 1763.

A. F. Macfie

Allan Fullerton Macfie was the dominant figure of that eventful tournament held at Hoylake in April, 1885. The idea, mooted by Thomas Owen Potter at a Council Meeting of the Royal Liverpool Golf Club, resolved that 'a Tournament open to all Amateur golfers should be held at Hoylake in the Spring Meeting Week of 1885.' The Committee appointed to oversee the event consisted of James Cullen, B. Hall Blyth, James Mansfield, John Dun, J. Logan White, F. C. Crawford, Charles D. Brown, T. O. Potter and Horace Hutchinson. Little did these nine gentlemen realise what the future would be for this competition which attracted 48 entries from the Clubs of the Royal Liverpool, Royal and Ancient, Blackheath, Royal Wimbledon, the Honourable Company of Edinburgh Golfers, New Club, North Berwick, Glasgow, Earlsferry and Elie, Dalhousie, Carnoustie, Worcestershire and London Scottish. The entrance fee was fixed at one guinea and two prizes were donated by the Royal Liverpool Golf Club. All was harmony and accord except for a technical nicety as to what constituted an *amateur*, or for that matter a clearer definition of a *professional*. The query had arisen because of an entry received from Douglas Rolland.

After finishing second to Jack Simpson in the Open Championship at Prestwick in 1884, Rolland had accepted prize money. By so doing he had broken the rule forbidding an amateur to receive a money prize when competing against professionals. The ruling was straightforward, until it was pointed out that some years earlier at an Open championship, John Ball as a lad had finished in the money-winning list and had accepted the prize of ten shillings. Technically the Rolland issue was comparable, but the possibility of Ball losing his amateur status because of this boyish mistake seemed absurd. Hutchinson anticipated that the Committee would reject Rolland's entry, but did not want to become involved, particularly as Rolland was rated his main opponent, so he begged leave to resign before the vote was taken. The entry was disallowed and as Ball's slip had occurred before he was sixteen, his amateur status deemed intact.

In the tournament, byes were not eliminated in the first round so there was only one semi-final. John Ball Tertius began his championship career by beating Colonel Kennard by 8 and 7. His father, John Ball Jr, also won his match against G. A. Gilroy, which meant that father and son met in the third round, youth winning on the sixteenth green. In the fourth round, Allan Macfie had a tough match against De Zoete and won only after extra holes when Macfie holed the Rushes in one, a victory which ensured a place in the semi-final in which he received a bye. The other semi-final between Horace Hutchinson and John Ball Tertius was a fluctuating affair. Ball, two up at the turn, looked the stronger player, but Hutchinson rallied, became dormy two, only to lose the seventeenth, where he drove out-of-bounds. He made no mistake at the eighteenth. His iron shot was dead and meant a win by two holes. Hutchinson was expected to crush Macfie in the final, but the Scot refused to be overawed. He won the first four holes and trounced Hutchinson by 7 and 6 on the twelfth green.

Afterwards, in response to a request made in January 1886 by Hall Blyth, the Hoylake captain, to the Royal and Ancient Golf Club, it was decided that a competition should be held over three Links in rotation, St Andrews, Hoylake and Prestwick. A piece of plate valued at £100 was bought with money subscribed by the twenty-four leading Clubs, the winner to receive a Gold

Medal. The outcome was the staging of the first Amateur Championship on the Old Course, St Andrews, in September 1886. There were ten matches in the first round, sixteen in the second. Macfie lost to J. E. Laidlay in the third round, who in turn was beaten by Ball Tertius in the next. Horace Hutchinson defeated H. A. Lamb in the final by 7 and 6, over eighteen holes. The 36 holes test did not come in until 1896.

After World War I, the Royal and Ancient Golf Club ruled that the 1885 Tournament at Hoylake should be recognised as the first Amateur Championship, which meant that A. F. Macfie became canonised as the first Amateur Champion, a recognition the Scot valued immensely. He was a familiar figure in St Andrews for many years, walking slowly across the Old Course, cap well down over his eyes, with drooping moustache and cleek in hand. As a golfer, his game lacked length. He used to say that he had never been over the Swilcan Burn in two shots at the first, but short game accuracy more than compensated. Caddies arriving early would find the fairway littered with balls left behind by Macfie, who practised tirelessly, after he had given up in the fading light of the previous evening. The first Amateur Champion was a member of the Royal and Ancient Golf Club for 61 years.

Allan Macfie, the first Amateur Champion and member of the Royal and Ancient Golf Club for 61 years. Although handicapped by deafness Macfie showed a lively interest in the game up to the end of his life.

Ted Ray

In 1912 Ted Ray won the Open Championship at Muirfield. He did so in characteristic fashion. A prodigious smiter, tall and powerfully built, he took no half-measures. He put every ounce of his considerable weight into the stroke, but a distinct forward lunge of the body often invited wayward shots. Cartoonists used to show him hacking his way out of a forest of bents and whins. His style was rough-hewn, but had definite rhythm in the swing. His recipe is remembered in an oft-quoted answer to one of his pupils who was trying to get more length to his drives: 'Hit it a bloody sight harder, mate.' One of his regrets was that Open Championship success eluded him at St Andrews, which he regarded with rare affection. Those who can look back over many years of championship golf will remember Ray walking across the Old Course with hat carelessly placed on the back of his head and puffing clouds of smoke from his favourite pipe. He looked so delightfully casual, and this happy-go-lucky streak seemed on the surface to run through his game as he wielded his niblick in the rough. The appearance was deceptive. Underneath, Ted Ray was a formidable golfer whose skill is preserved for posterity in the records. But it was when he used to describe the early years of his life that his robust humour came to the fore. He was born in 1877 and used to say that he swung a club as soon as he could walk. His first club was made by his father. The head was one of the wooden pins used by fishermen for mending nets. With the help of a red-hot poker, a hole was made into which was fitted a thorn stick and the club was complete. Ray used to refer to it as the first of the socket type of club. The next stage came when he fashioned his own clubs with a pocket knife from any suitable wood he found in the lanes. His juvenile career ended when he became the owner of a real golf club. He would compare his golf beginnings with those of Sandy Herd, who adapted shinty sticks cut from Strathtyrum Woods, using champagne corks found in a refuse heap behind the Royal and Ancient Golf Club as golf balls, weight being added by inserting screw-nails into the corks. Ray said he would have liked to play Sandy Herd and Laurie Auchterlonie on their childhood links of the cobblestoned streets of St Andrews, with lamp-posts for flags at the cathedral end of North Street. The daydreams of all three boys came true in the Open Championships of America and this country.

Ted Ray was a giant personality in every sense of the word, almost hewn out of granite. His style was individual to a remarkable degree. He was essentially a natural player, the artistic side of his game being overshadowed by the sheer efficiency of his methods. His long driving and extraordinary powers of recovery became legendary. He was a St Andrean by adoption and would have been proud to be of the rich company of St Andrews characters.

Lord Balfour

'A tolerable day, a tolerable green, a tolerable opponent supply, or ought to supply, all that any reasonably constituted human being should require in the way of entertainment.' So said Arthur Balfour. It was certainly true in his case. No mean golfer, he never missed a chance to play. His enthusiasm was infectious. It prompted G. K. Chesterton to comment, 'Golf came with a rush over the Border like the blue-bonnets and grew fashionable largely because Arthur Balfour was the fashion.' During his term of office as Chief Secretary for Ireland in 1887, he insisted on sampling the Irish links in spite of threats to his life after the Phoenix Park murders in 1887, and relied on the protection given by two detectives. Nerves were never a worry. This was evident in the early photograph of him as Captain of the Royal and Ancient Golf Club. The ball is flighting down the first fairway of the Old Course and he is watched by his partner, Graham Murray, the 1892 Captain, with an appreciative Tom Morris applauding in the background.

In appearance Arthur Balfour never varied. His taste became the golfing norm. It was not always so in St Andrews. A Minute dated 4 August 1780 reads: 'This day the Society took into their consideration that their golfing jackets are in bad condition and have agreed that they shall all have new ones – viz., red with yellow buttons. The undermentioned gentlemen have likewise agreed to have an uniform frock – viz., a buff colour with a red cap. The coat to be half-lapelled according to the pattern produced, the button white.' The signatures were the eleven members who decked themselves in 'dyed garments from Bozrah', led by the Earl of Balcarres. Four years later variations were announced, '. . . a red coat with a dark-blue velvet cape, with plain white buttons, with an embroidered club and ball of silver on each side of the cape, with two large buttons on the sleeves.' Colonel R. T. Boothby, the 1921 Captain, attempted to revive the custom, advocating a plain blue coat with the Club buttons which he used to wear. All very colourful, but not as tasteful as the conservative touch of Lord Balfour which blended into the St Andrews landscape.

Lord Balfour took up golf when he became minister in charge of Scottish affairs in 1886. Tom Dunn, North Berwick professional, gave him his first lessons.

James Robb

James Robb became interested in golf while studying at Madras College in St Andrews. The style he developed had little in common with the traditional St Andrews swing, being short and rapid, relying on the strength of forearm and wrist. On the greens he preferred a putting cleek, which he used to great effect. He won the British Amateur Championship in 1906, was twice runner-up, and semi-finalist on four occasions. For four years he was a member of the Scottish team in the international matches against England. After winning innumerable St Andrews trophies, Robb left to take up a banking appointment in Prestwick and for several years enjoyed golfing successes in the West of Scotland before retiring to St Andrews, becoming an active member of the artisan St Andrews Club.

Edward Blackwell

Edward Blackwell was a true product of St Andrews. He was born in 1866 in a house on the edge of the Old Course. At the age of five, he was given his first golf club, a crudely made driver lacking lead and bone. Three years later he played in a competition for the pupils of Dr Browning's school. The winner was Walter Blackwell with 104. Edward came second with 108. At Glenalmond he took advantage of the small course laid out on the cricket fields where play was permitted from summer to Christmas. During school holidays, it was back to St Andrews where his golfing friend was Freddie Tait, who received a half. Blackwell's bag was not overstocked. It consisted of three clubs – driver, iron and cleek, which served as a putter and led to the habit of stabbing the ball instead of following through. Nevertheless, it did not stop him playing off scratch at 18.

In 1885, the Glenalmond chapter closed and Blackwell returned to St Andrews. Shortly afterwards, H. B. Simpson of Brunton arranged a 36-hole match between Blackwell and Jack Simpson, the Open Champion. Edward won by a single hole. A few days later he left for the United States, where for six years he never visited a golf course. Despite the long lay-off, he returned home and won the William IV Medal at the Autumn Meeting with a record card of 82. A further five years in America followed, again without his touching a golf club. Returning to St Andrews, he resumed winning by taking the Calcutta Cup from plus two. That became plus five when he went to Pau in the Spring of 1898 and, in partnership with Charles Hutchings, won the Kilmaine Cup for Pau against Biarritz.

Feats such as these were soon forgotten. Instead Edward Blackwell was remembered for the 1904 Amateur Championship at Sandwich, when he lost in the final to W. J. Travis whose putting was inspired. Blackwell disagreed that the title disappeared on the greens. He blamed the forward tees which favoured the shorter-driving American, who otherwise would not have been able to match his opponent's power golf. Horace Hutchinson left a contemporary pen-portrait: 'Standing above six feet in height, his physique shows the very perfection of strength. Not only is he well endowed but his strength is something altogether out of the common; and it is strength of that special quality that is capable of being exerted in rapid movement. It is doubtless this union of activity and power, combined with the ideal orthodoxy of his style, that gives him his tremendous length of drive.' Judging by old photographs, it is questionable whether purists would agree with Hutchinson's idea of orthodoxy. Blackwell was certainly individualistic in style. The club was held in the palm of both hands, with the left thumb outside, which clearly allowed the hands to slide on the shaft during the swing. At the top of the swing his right elbow was raised at an unusual height. It was a St Andrews swing, though the club was rarely below the horizontal behind the back. Blackwell never had professional coaching. He was taught the rudiments by his father, who was a keen golfer. After that he developed his own style, which made him one of the longest drivers. In 1892, he reached the green of the 520-yard fifth hole at St Andrews in two shots, with the wind slightly against, in a match with Major Robert Bethune. Turning around he played the same hole going in and again found the green with his second . . . more than a thousand yards in four shots with a guttie.

Blackwell also drove from the eighteenth tee on the Old Course to the steps on the left of the green. His longest single drive measured by tape was in 1892 from the seventeenth tee – that was 366 yards with a gutta-percha ball. Blackwell's short game improved when he switched to an aluminium putter, but it worked best on the Old Course. On other greens he had difficulty in judging distances, but this did not stop him playing longer for Scotland than any other man.

Edward Blackwell was a colourful link with the golfing past, though his claim to have known Strath was a trifle forced. It had nothing to do with golf. Apparently Strath fancied Blackwell's nurse and most of their courting took place with the infant Edward in the perambulator, which must have left a somewhat hazy recollection of the legendary St Andrews golfer born in 1836.

Professor Peter Guthrie Tait

Peter Guthrie Tait, professor of philosophy and mathematician at Edinburgh University, had a life-long affection for St Andrews. From 1868, he stayed there every summer for some 30 years and was a member of the Royal and Ancient Golf Club for 36 years. His enthusiasm for golf was remarkable. Five rounds a day over the Old Course meant a start at about 6 am, a routine which would tax the stamina of the fittest and was certainly too much for the caddies who worked on a shift basis. John Low aptly described the Professor as 'the oldest boy and the youngest old man we ever knew.' Low, who was one of the founders of the Oxford and Cambridge Golfing Society and Chairman of the Rules of Golf Committee for twenty years, also recorded one of the lighter moments of Tait's golfing activities: . . . In 1871 the meeting of the British Association was held in Edinburgh, the Professor being President of Section A. After the proceedings were finished some of the most distinguished members of this assembly accompanied him to St Andrews. Among them were Huxley, Helmholtz, Andrews and Sylvester . . . It is the dinner hour and the professor proposes to the company that a round may be played with phosphorescent balls. When the proper arrangements have been made the party assemble at the first teeing ground. To this match come the Professor and his lady, Huxley, keen on the humour of the thing, Professor Crum Brown and another friend. The idea is a success; the balls glisten in the grass and advertise their situation; the players make strokes which surprise their opponents and apprise themselves of hitherto unknown powers. All goes well till the burn is passed, and Professor Crum Brown's hand is found to be aflame; with difficulty his burning glove is unbuttoned and the saddened group return to the Professor's rooms, where Huxley dresses the wounds.'

Viewing the game from a scientific point of view, Tait was puzzled by the anomalous behaviour of a golf ball, noting that without spin its flight was limited and that a ball's centre of gravity rarely coincided with the ball's actual centre. He stated dogmatically that the carry of a golfball would be about 190 yards, only to have his famous golfing son, Freddie Tait, disprove the theory by driving a ball 341 yards 9 inches at the thirteenth on the Old Course, the gutta having a carry of 250 yards.

The Professor died on 4 July 1901. Members of the Royal and Ancient Golf Club paid tribute to his memory at a meeting two days later.

Andrew Lang

When Theodore Roosevelt, President of the United States, gave the Romanes Lecture in the Sheldonian Theatre at Oxford in 1910, he was asked whom he would like to meet. His list consisted of Rudyard Kipling, Gilbert Murray, Kenneth Grahame, Sir Charles Oman and Andrew Lang. The last named was one of St Andrews' most distinguished literary figures, a versatile Victorian and Edwardian critic, poet of quality, translator who combined scholarship with fluent style and possessed an imaginative knack of capturing the intangible world of the story-book in reality. His book *Prince Prigio* ranks with *Alice* and *The Rose and the Ring*. Literary fame can be short-lived and though at the time of his death, Lang was an important figure in contemporary letters, today he is little known. It was partly his fault. Shy and reserved, he left the wish that no one should write his life, and his widow destroyed papers and letters. Only his closest friend, Rider Haggard, published a few of his letters in the autobiography *The Days of My Life*.

In a long career, Andrew Lang achieved many honours and distinctions, but it was always to St Andrews that he returned. Born in Selkirk on 31 March 1844, Lang's first link with St Andrews came in 1853 when his mother's brother, William Young Sellar became assistant to the Professor of Greek in the University, later succeeding to the Greek Chair. Educated at Selkirk Grammar School, Lang matriculated in 1861 at St Andrews University and entered into St Leonard's Hall, which he recorded 'was in effect something between an Oxford Hall and a master's house at a public school, rather more like the latter than the former. We were more free than schoolboys, not so free as undergraduates.' This Hall was based on Principal Forbes's ideas, best described by Principal Shairp: 'In St Andrews, as in other Scottish Universities, it had long been customary for students to live where they chose in lodgings in the town. In old times, St Andrews had been resorted to as a place of education by the sons of many persons in the higher ranks. This had, however, entirely ceased more than thirty years before Principal Forbes' advent to St Andrews. Professors who had once been in the habit of taking boarders had ceased to do so, and the general set of the educational tide southward had borne from St Andrews to England almost all who could afford to go thither. It seemed to Principal Forbes, and others, that the idea of a University, as originally held in Scotland, was not fulfilled, unless it contained students of all ranks; and it occurred to them whether, by providing a fitting place of residence under proper superintendence, some of those who has left it, to the loss of the University, and of themselves, might not be lured back.'

Thirty years after his first matriculation, Lang returned to St Andrews. With his wife, he spent the winter months in a house on the cliff edge near the castle ruins. In 1885, the University had conferred on him the Honorary Degree of Doctor of Laws. Three years later he was appointed first Gifford Lecturer, in all delivering 40 lectures none of which was published, though he based *The Making of Religion* on them. In the same year the Royal and Ancient Golf Club agreed to an unusual election. Lang was a candidate for membership, but as he was going to St Andrews to deliver the Gifford Lectures and it would be some time before a ballot was scheduled, the Committee 'in respect of Mr Lang's distinguished literary attainments agreed to admit Mr Lang as a visitor without payment till a Ballot took place'.

Another pen-portrait of Andrew Lang was left by his

friend Sir Herbert Maxwell in his *Evening Memories*. The setting is the Quadrangle of the United College, the occasion the Quincentenary Celebrations of 1911: 'In the brilliant September sunshine, gowns and hoods of scarlet and white, orange and blue, purple and green, presented the appearance of a great parterre crowded with huge, gaudy flowers. Making my way through this august assembly, I was not well pleased to find Andrew Lang seated on the grass in a suit of mustard coloured tweed, over which he had donned a shabby gown of black bombazine and a red hood all awry. I felt displeased, and told him so, for surely he, of all men, should have been more scrupulous in doing honour to ". . . the little city, grey and sere."'

As regards Lang's interest in sport, angling was always high on the list. Cricket appealed; in fact he once said that his idea of heaven was a place where he would always find a good wicket and never exceed the age of 24. Golf was to be taken more seriously. In the first chapter which he wrote for the Badminton *Golf* in 1890 his views were clear: 'To write the history of golf as it should be done demands a thorough study of all Scottish Acts of Parliament, Kirk Sessions records, memoirs and in fact of Scottish literature, legislation, and history from the beginning of time . . . A young man must do it, and he will be so ancient before he finishes toil that he will scarce see the flag on the short hole at St Andrews from the tee.' He was fascinated by the origin of the game. The earliest references to golf and the Dutch *kolven* are usually dated about the middle of the 15th century, but Andrew Lang referred in his Lexicon of Low Latin to various references to *chole* from legal documents of 1353 and 1357 which is a century earlier than any references to the other two games. He also put forward interesting suggestions about the golf balls used during the time of the Stuart kings. He believed they were made of turned boxwood, similar to the balls used in *chole* and *pall-mall*. He put forward as confirmation of this theory a despatch of the reign of James VI, in which the writer, describing the siege of a castle belonging to the Earl of Orkney, told of cannon balls bursting into fragments 'like golf balls' against the walls. Had they been feather balls, they would have split open, not broken into pieces.

But not all his writings on golf were serious. He penned several light-hearted sketches about the game, like *Herodotus at St Andrews* and *Dr Johnson on the Links* which appeared in *College Echoes*, the University magazine, and later published in *A Batch of Golfing Papers*. Horace Hutchinson was complimentary in part when he wrote, 'Lang writes well of golf, so far as a man can write well of a game which he cannot play at all. Even a stroke a hole handicap would have complimented him too highly!' The stricture was too unkind, for however badly he played there was no doubt that Lang enjoyed his timid attempts to master the Old Course. He recorded how he fared in a foursome with ladies at St Andrews in 1873: 'Next morning early I fled, into the wilds of Athole, with a price on my head, while my male opponent (English) put Tweed between himself and mischief. We only retreated just in time: our partners were left to the female tongues of St Andrews. I was much the oldest of the nefarious foursome, and ought to have known better; any way my side lost, and I had to pay the stakes. But what an awful example of iniquity did I thoughtlessly set!' Women golfers in St Andrews at that time confined themselves to the short course. The St Andrews Ladies' Golf Club had been formed in 1867 with a programme that included Spring and Autumn

Meetings with prizes of a Gold Medal and a Silver Cross.

Lang was not shy to criticise, particularly the establishment of commercial universities. In March 1899 there was such an instance: 'As to St Andrews, whose only commerce is potatoes and golf balls, we might found the Morris Chair of Golf-ball making, scientifically heated. I fancy that I hear Professor Morris discoursing on the Laws of Flight of Spherical Bodies with reference to the theory of Professor Tait and the experiments of Mr Frederick Tait and Mr Blackwell. Professor Morris's course would far excel in popularity those of the Professors of Greek, Latin and Philosophy.' He followed Freddie Tait's golfing career with interest. In the introduction to John Low's biography of the Scottish player, he describes in detail Tait's famous drive on the Old Course: 'I remember Tait coming into the Club and asking whether it was worth while to measure a drive he had made. He had in fact "overpowered" the Heathery Hole, the thirteenth as you come in on the right-hand course. The drive has been disputed, and I only narrate what I remember. Perhaps my recollection is inaccurate. He was playing behind his brother Willie, and, when the brother and partner had played their second, Freddie's ball flew over their heads, and lighted on the long narrow table-land which there crosses the links. Freddie, on approaching the hole, could not find his ball, and, I think, gave up the hole, and then found his ball about hole-high. The day was of a light frost, brilliantly sunny, and with the faintest flicker of air, no breeze. I remember seeing Mr Tait measuring the distance to the place where the ball was found, and I think the whole extent was about 350 yards, the "carry" being about 250 yards.'

The closing years of Lang's life were marked by failing health and threatened blindness, which he accepted with uncomplaining stoicism. Sisters Lady King-Stewart and Ella Christie recalled his attitude in *A Long Look at Life*: 'When I was staying with them at St Andrews for a few days Mrs Lang confided to me that, as he wished to be buried there, she must see about reserving a bit of ground; so, while he and I were exploring the historic "bits", she went off on her errand and, after lunch, informed me what she had done. When A.L. was told, all he said was: "You've placed me terribly near the gasworks." "Yes, Andrew, but within sound of the sea", was her ready reply.'

Andrew Lang died of *angina pectoris* at Banchory on 20 July 1912. He was buried 'within sound of the sea' in the Cathedral grounds at St Andrews. A year later a memorial mural tablet of a bronze casting framed in Timos marble was placed in the College Chapel. Below his name are some Greek lines composed by his friend, Alexander Shewan. Translated they read, 'A long farewell to thee, sea-washed seat of holy Andrew, pleasant to me in life and ever greatly longed for; and now art thou ever dearer, little town, in that thou gavest me, out-worn, rest eternal after toil.'

Bernard Darwin

Bernard Darwin once described writing about sport as a 'job into which men drift, since no properly constituted parent would agree to his son starting his career in that way. Having tried something else which bores them they take to this thing which is lightly esteemed by the outside world, but which satisfies in them some possibly childish but certainly romantic feeling.' Golfing journalists on the whole are realists about their own. They have no illusions about what they are doing. They are certainly not writing for posterity. All daily writing is, or should be, ephemeral, and most ephemeral of all is writing on sport.

Darwin was an exception. Born at Downe, Kent on 7 September 1876, his early background was Eton, Cambridge and the Temple. In World War I he spent two-and-a-half years at Salonica. Although a barrister and a fully qualified solicitor, he found the lure of golf too strong, not solely as a scribe, but as a competitor. He was in the English team against Scotland on eight occasions, and played for England against America in the first Walker Cup match in 1922 at Long Island, when the British captain was taken ill. He was twice semi-finalist in the Amateur Championship, won the President's Putter in 1922 and the Worplesdon Foursomes in 1933 with Joyce Wethered. His first contribution to *The Times* was in 1907 and for the next 46 years his column appeared in that newspaper and *Country Life*. He also wrote some twenty books.

Bernard Darwin, although a barrister by profession, found the lure of golf too strong and was golfing correspondent for *The Times* for 46 years.

On some topics Darwin was partisan and unashamed, particularly when it came to university golf, rugby and the Boat Race. Some people regarded such bias as madness, but it was an honest frenzy and in your own kingdom he had the right. The Darwinian kingdom was very much a world on its own. Darwin wielded his pen with the touch of Lamb and the vividness of Hazlitt. This rare blend of fluent English and beguiling charm with an occasional touch of gusto made him one of the top prose writers of the twentieth century. Prosaic material had been transformed into literary journalism. In 1937, Bernard Darwin received the CBE. Three years earlier, he attained the highest position the game can offer, Captaincy of the Royal and Ancient Golf Club. It was an honour richly deserved. His familiar quotation came from *The Golfing Manual* of 1857, 'Golf, thou art a gentle sprite, I owe thee much.' Generations of golfers could say the same of Bernard.

The name of Auchterlonie has been known and respected in St Andrews for many years. Of the five brothers, all of whom were keen golfers, two were outstanding. The eldest, Laurence, was born in St Andrews in 1868. He decided to work in America and for several years was professional at the Glenview Club. His eventful year was 1902. He entered for the United States Open Championship at Garden City, Long Island. Increased prize-money attracted an entry of 90 with the bait of $200 for the winner and $970 shared among the first ten places. Auchterlonie liked the new ball which had been developed jointly by Goodrich Company and a Cleveland amateur named Coburn Haskell. The hard rubber core had added some twenty yards to a drive. Auchterlonie's four rounds of 78–78–74–77 not only won the US Open title, but for the first time the winner had broken 80 in all four rounds. In second place came Walter J. Travis, the leading American amateur of that time and designer of the Garden City course. A couple of years later, Travis became the first American to win the British Amateur Championship. Laurence Auchterlonie returned home to St Andrews and finished second in the Scottish Professional Championship of 1919.

Willie Auchterlonie, born in St Andrews in 1872, played in the Open for the first time at the age of sixteen, when Jack Burns won the title over the Old Course from an entry of 53 with an aggregate of 171. Five years later, it was his turn to win the Championship with a total of 322. Auchterlonie's equipment consisted of a set of seven clubs he had made himself. Provided a player had mastered the technique of the half, three-quarter and full shots, they were more than adequate. Not long afterwards, he began the famous St Andrews clubmaking company. In that 1893 open his winning aggregate of

322 had been followed by J. E. Laidlay – 324; Sandy Herd – 325; Hugh Kirkaldy – 326; Andrew Kirkaldy – also 326; with Old Tom Morris on 383. Virtually the same entry went to Newcastle, Co. Down for the Irish Open Championship. Willie Auchterlonie was again the winner with 322; Herd – 325; Hugh and Andrew Kirkaldy tieing with 326; J. H. Taylor – 333; Ben Sayers on 335; Harry Vardon – 344; Tom Vardon – 345; and Old Tom on 383. Auchterlonie was appointed Royal and Ancient professional in September 1935 and carried out his duties with courteous efficiency. He laid out the eighteen-hole Jubilee Course at St Andrews, which was opened in 1946. In 1950 he accepted Honorary Membership of the Royal and Ancient Golf Club, along with James Braid and J. H. Taylor. He died in 1964 aged 91. The Auchterlonie tradition was continued when his son, Laurie, the expert clubmaker, was appointed professional to the Royal and Ancient Golf Club.

Willie Auchterlonie (left) won the Open Championship in 1893 whilst Laurie took the US Open title in 1902.

Lord Brabazon of Tara

Of all the Captains of the Royal and Ancient Golf Club, Lord Brabazon of Tara was one of the most remarkable. He had achieved so much in so many different fields that the term *unique* might be correctly applied. It is hard to describe his influence to anyone who did not feel the impact of his personality. He was the personification of thoroughness. He could be as crude and direct as a newsreel, and had a fierce line in glares and all the other signs of the grim Protestant, plus a booming voice to emphasise a point. His imagination, free from the shackles of ordinary workaday citizens, moved in several worlds.

Much of what he achieved has vanished through the sieve of memory, but he will be remembered as holding the Aviator's Certificate No. 1 of the Fédération Aéronautique Internationale dated 8 March 1910. Some thirty years later he marked that occasion by securing a personal car number, FLY 1. He won the £1,000 prize offered by the *Daily Mail* for a circular flight of one mile by flying a hotch-potch of a flying machine at an average height of 40 feet. He won the Circuit des Ardennes in 1907 in a Minerva, and was not only one of the earliest riders on the Cresta toboggan run, but the oldest when he was in his seventies. In World War I he pioneered aerial photography.

In the House of Commons Brab left many stories, such as his reference to the Opposition as 'a lot of inverted Micawbers waiting for something to turn down.' In another place he dismissed the Archbishop of Canterbury's comments on finance as 'talking through his mitre'. During the war Brabazon was Minister of Transport, then in charge of Aircraft Production. He was also President of the Royal Institution. His value on a golf committee was that of a goad, highlighting the inefficiency of many of his colleagues, but he was always ready for a light aside. I recall when he sat next to me at an Executive Meeting of the English Golf Union. He offered me a cigar, then a cigarette, followed by tobacco and finally snuff before accepting the fact that I was a non-smoker.

Brabazon caused consternation among the caddies at St Andrews when he took the first caddie car around the Old Course. Their concern was understandable – it was a threat to their livelihood. Not long afterwards the post of Links caddie-master was discontinued, but has happily now been restored by the Links Trust.

With such a remarkable background, he should have matched up on another momentous occasion. At 8 am in front of past Captains and an assembly of local citizens and visitors, he drove himself down the first fairway as Captain of the Royal and Ancient Golf Club. Instead of a crashing drive, the ball scuttled along the ground in the wrong direction and came to rest long before the waiting caddies could retrieve it. Even so, it did not spoil his day. Nothing ever did. This attitude was mirrored in Brabazon's autobiography in which he wrote, 'When I look back on my life and try to decide out of what I have got more actual pleasure, I have no doubt at all that I have got more out of golf than anything else.'

Lord Brabazon congratulating the Americans on their dramatic victory in the 1953 Ryder Cup match. On the platform are Lord Lyle, Fred Daly, Dai Rees and Commander Roe.

Adieu to St Andrews

St Andrews ! they say that thy glories are gone,
That thy streets are deserted, thy castles o'erthrown;
If thy glories *be* gone, they are only, methinks,
As it were, by enchantment, transferr'd to thy Links.
Though thy streets be not, as of yore, full of prelates,
Of abbots and monks, and of hot-headed zealots,
Let none judge us rashly, or blame us as scoffers,
When we say that instead there are Links full of Golfers,
With more of good heart and good feeling among them
Than the abbots, the monks, and the zealots who sung them;
We have red coats and bonnets, we've putters and clubs;
The green has its bunkers, its hazards, and *rubs*;
At the long hole anon we have biscuits and beer,
And the Hebes who sell it give zest to the cheer;
If this makes not up for the pomp and the splendour
Of mitres, and murders, and mass – we'll surrender;
If Golfers and caddies be not better neighbours
Than abbots and soldiers, with crosses and sabres,
Let such fancies remain with the fool who thinks,
While we toast old St Andrews, its Golfers, and Links.

George Fullarton Carnegie of Pitarrow (1813).

ST ANDREWS
AN APPRECIATION

Few golf historians knew St Andrews and the Old Course so intimately as Sir Guy Campbell. His zest for detail of the past never flagged. It was encyclopaedic in its embrace. This great-grandson of Robert Chambers summed-up his appreciation of the home of golf in the poem, *The Old Course Speaks*:

I have heard the North Sea
Ceaselessly withdrawing,
Foot by foot receding,
Through the Ages as they spent;
Adding to my Loanings,
Gracious ground for Golfers,
Spread far for their content.

Gulls and Terns and Curlews
Left me rich guano;
Sand and Silt and sea-wrack –
The tilth that made my sward.
Cunningies then cropped it,
And foxes followed after,
Fashioning my fairways
And Greens for Golf's reward.

Winter, Spring and Summer,
Autumn, in their seasons;
Snow and haar and sunshine
With wind, and wave, and rain,
Tempered my whole being,
Brought me growth and vigour,
Bent, and whin, and heather
To pattern my campaign.

Countless feet have worn me –
Children, men and women;
Multitudes have scarred me;
Come frost, come wet, come shine.
Service without measure,
Healing for my treasure, –
I renew at leisure.
The secret still is mine.

Through long generations
I have watched Golf's pageant;
I have known its Powers,
And Princes in their prime,
Vieing with each other
One year to another,
Yet for many changes
The Art is one with Time.

So it was and has been;
So it is and will be.
I abide unchallenged,
And peerless is my Name.
History behind me,
I give all who find me
Welcome and a Blessing,
To the Glory of the Game.

205

DATES OF CONSEQUENCE
IN THE HISTORY OF ST ANDREWS

1759   Reference to stroke play in Rules
1764   Introduction of 18 holes
1787   Stymie rule introduced
1797   Links sold by Town Council
1817   St Andrews Thistle Club founded
1834   Society of Golfers changed to Royal and Ancient Golf Club
1838   Penalty rule for lost ball
1843   St Andrews Golf Club inaugurated as Mechanics Club
1848   Gutta-percha ball introduced
1851   Railway line laid beside the Links
1854   Royal and Ancient Clubhouse built
1858   Allan Robertson became the first professional
1865   Tom Morris became first professional to Royal and Ancient
1867   First Ladies Club at St Andrews
1873   Open Championship played first time at St Andrews
1876   Amalgamation of Royal and Ancient with Union Club
1886   Left-handed course used for only time in a championship
1893   Willie Auchterlonie won Open Championship
1895   New Course opened
1908   Death of Tom Morris
1914   Eden Course opened
1922   Prince of Wales played in as Captain of the Royal and Ancient
1929   Steel shafts legalised by Royal and Ancient
1930   Duke of York played in as Captain of R. and A.
1933   Spectators charged gate-money for first time
1938   Great Britain's first victory in Walker Cup match
1946   Crowd control system introduced
1950   First Commonwealth Tournament
1951   Stymie abolished
1951   Francis Ouimet became first American to be Captain of the Royal and Ancient
1955   Open Championship televised for first time
1967   Sunday play in tournaments allowed for first time
1969   Traffic lights on 1st and 18th fairways

1970	Sunday practice allowed in Open
1972	Balgove course opened
1974	Links Trust and Links Management Committee formed
1977	Ladies Golf Union headquarters in St Andrews
1980	Rusack's Hotel bought by Links Trust
1982	Old Course Hotel bought by Frank Sheridan
1983	Old Course Golf and Country Club opened by Princess Anne

ACKNOWLEDGEMENTS

Colour illustrations are reproduced by kind permission of the following:

The Royal and Ancient Golf Club at St Andrews
Lawrence Levy, Yours In Sport
The Fishmongers' Company
Pietro Annigoni

All black and white photographs are by the author with the following exceptions:

Page 15, by Peter Adamson
Pages 101, 117, 120, 122, 123, 125, 126, 127, 130, 132, 135, 136, 141, 158, 159, 160, by H. W. Neale

The line drawings of the holes of the Old Course on pages 37 to 54 are reproduced by permission of BBC Publications.

The author, Louis T. Stanley.

INDEX

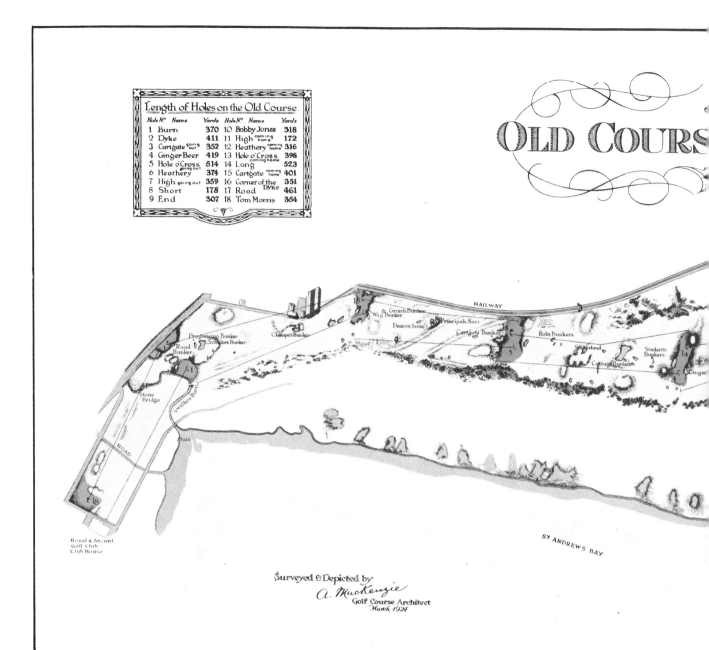

Length of Holes on the Old Course.

Hole Nº	Name	Yards	Hole Nº	Name	Yards
1	Burn	370	10	Bobby Jones	318
2	Dyke	411	11	High coming home	172
3	Cartgate going out	352	12	Heathery coming home	316
4	Ginger Beer	419	13	Hole o'Cross coming home	398
5	Hole o'Cross going out	514	14	Long	523
6	Heathery going out	374	15	Cartgate coming home	401
7	High going out	359	16	Corner of the Dyke	351
8	Short	178	17	Road	461
9	End	307	18	Tom Morris	354

OLD COURS

RAILWAY

Grants Bunker
Wig Bunker
Deacon Sime
Principals Nose
Cartgate Bunker
Robs Bunkers
Sutherland
Students Bunkers
Cottage Bunkers
Ginger

Cheape's Bunker
Stigue

Progressing Bunker
Scholars Bunker

Road Bunker

Stone Bridge
Swilken Burn

ROAD

St ANDREWS BAY

Royal & Ancient
Golf Club
Club House

Surveyed & Depicted by
A. MacKenzie
Golf Course Architect
March 1924